411815

Encounters with Florida's Endangered Wildlife

UNIVERSITY PRESS OF FLORIDA

Florida A&M University, Tallahassee
Florida Atlantic University, Boca Raton
Florida Gulf Coast University, Ft. Myers
Florida International University, Miami
Florida State University, Tallahassee
New College of Florida, Sarasota
University of Central Florida, Orlando
University of Florida, Gainesville
University of North Florida, Jacksonville
University of South Florida, Tampa
University of West Florida, Pensacola

Encounters with

Florida's Endangered Wildlife

Doug Alderson

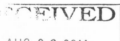
University Press of Florida
Gainesville / Tallahassee / Tampa / Boca Raton
Pensacola / Orlando / Miami / Jacksonville / Ft. Myers / Sarasota

Copyright 2010 by Doug Alderson
Printed in the United States of America. This book is printed on
Glatfelter Natures Book, a paper certified under the standards of the
Forestry Stewardship Council (FSC). It is a recycled stock that contains
30 percent post-consumer waste and is acid-free.

15 14 13 12 11 10   6 5 4 3 2 1

Library of Congress Cataloging-in-Publication Data
Alderson, Doug.
Encounters with florida's endangered wildlife/Doug Alderson.
p. cm.
Includes bibliographical references and index.
ISBN 978-0-8130-3476-8 (alk. paper)
1. Endangered species—Florida. I. Title.
QL84.22.F6A43 2010
591.68097599–dc22   2009044777

Photos by author unless otherwise noted. Frontispiece: Limpkin calling.

The University Press of Florida is the scholarly publishing agency
for the State University System of Florida, comprising Florida A&M
University, Florida Atlantic University, Florida Gulf Coast University,
Florida International University, Florida State University, New College
of Florida, University of Central Florida, University of Florida,
University of North Florida, University of South Florida,
and University of West Florida.

University Press of Florida
15 Northwest 15th Street
Gainesville, FL 32611-2079
http://www.upf.com

Contents

Preface

Over the years, my search for rare and endangered species has become a quest to go beyond ordinary and familiar boundaries.

I live in a wooded area south of Tallahassee. My five acres has lovely creatures—cardinals, squirrels, black racers, skinks, hawks . . . but I find myself yearning for the flash of panther fur at sunset, a black bear groping for grubs, the bold silhouette of a whooping crane overhead, and the distinctive double-knock rap of an ivory-billed woodpecker. Seeing these creatures on or near my property was possible only a century ago, but very unlikely today. And so I find myself searching for these and other uncommon creatures in Florida's clear waters and last wild places. When I find one, or a clear sign, I almost feel vindicated. Perhaps we are bringing our most destructive habits in check by simply allowing other species to live in their natural habitats.

Encounters with Florida's Endangered Wildlife combines adventure, natural history, and cultural history. You'll meet people who are working tirelessly on behalf of endangered species, and you'll also explore habitats that have become endangered. Some habitats, especially those on public lands, are actually improving because of management practices such as prescribed burning and restrictions on activities such as logging, and this bodes well for the many wildlife species that depend on them.

Although not encyclopedic in scope, this book features several species that are symbolic of wild Florida—the Florida panther, Florida black bear, whooping crane, Florida manatee, Florida scrub-jay, Florida's sea turtles, rare mussels and salamanders, and the ivory-billed woodpecker. Even if evidence of the ivory-bill remains inconclusive, protection of habitat for these animals will benefit countless other species, and our journeys into their domain will have an added richness and mystery.

And I would be remiss if I did not discuss the changing wildlife map of Florida because of climate change and the introduction of exotic species such as Burmese pythons. But don't worry. This is not a doom-and-gloom book. There is a concerted effort to address both concerns as we seek to restore and protect healthy wildlife populations into the future.

What Is Gone

North Florida's Wakulla Springs is a peaceful place late in the day, when tour boats have docked and throngs of local boys have finished impressing bikini-clad girls with their cannonballs and jackknives off the two-story diving tower. Then, I can ascend the platform, quietly perch near the edge, and become lost in the dizzying depths below. Few places are more spectacular than Wakulla Springs when the water is clear.

Alligators cruise in to reclaim their domain. Schools of mullet and bream swim by along with monster catfish and the more predatory bass and gar. Primitive anhingas dive underwater in hopes of spearing fish with sharp bills, their serpentine necks threading through the water. Manatees swim around the spring bowl on occasion as they have for millennia. With noisy crowds absent, Wakulla Springs has a different feel, reminding me of when I walked through a zoo after closing and listened—awestruck—to echoing cries, roars, and howls of animals now free to be themselves.

Wildness is difficult to completely subdue, especially at Wakulla.

If Wakulla Springs were an oracle, it would seem the perfect

North Florida's Wakulla Springs houses the remains of many prehistoric animals.

place to reveal Florida's origins. Before the age of dinosaurs, an ancient land slowly sank beneath what is now the Atlantic Ocean and Gulf of Mexico. For millions of years, there was water, simply water. And whether the Creek Indian tale of a sea turtle mounding up land higher and higher until it rose above water is true, or whether Noah landed his ark on a bluff along the Apalachicola River during the Great Flood, as a local preacher once purported, land began to reappear in what is now Florida.

Early shorelines left behind giant dunes that formed sand ridges and dry uplands. Rivers carved their own paths through the new land, snaking back and forth over millennia and leaving behind wetlands and vast clay deposits. The dead life from the ancient seas formed layers of porous limestone, greater than 10,000 feet thick in places. Over time, freshwater mixed with decaying vegetation to form a mild acidic solution that slowly dissolved limestone. The result was a labyrinth of caves and fissures, a honeycomb through which underground rivers could pass and emerge as springs.

Sometimes, I visualize myself journeying into Wakulla's depths, much like a shaman who ventures into the lower world. I can see myself surrounded by water, clear blue water, the caves illuminated by some pure ethereal light.

Cave divers describe an array of nocturnal fishes—bullheads, suckers, and white catfish. There are also sleek American eels that are halfway on an incredible round-trip journey from the Sargasso Sea, east of the Bahamas, where they were born. Deep inside Wakulla's dark caverns are blind cave crayfish. More delicate in body than their cousins on the surface, they are believed to be capable of living for more than a hundred years. Albino survivors.

Remains of extinct animals are found inside the caves, too, so many that one underwater room has been labeled "the megafauna mausoleum." Most were from the Pleistocene Epoch more than 10,000 years ago. Prehistoric elephants—huge mammoths and mastodons—along with artifacts and remains of early Paleo people who hunted the prehistoric beasts, lay entombed 250 feet below the surface. Other likely bones include those of giant lions and jaguars, tiger-sized saber-toothed cats, beavers as big as black bears, ground sloths 16 feet in length, and 10-foot-tall sharp-beaked flightless birds that probably ate both plants and small animals—all relics of the Pleistocene era. Remains of giant armadillos and tortoises, bears and wolves, long-horned bison, antelope, llama-sized camels, horses, tapirs, capybaras, and peccaries may also be preserved. It is a march of history only a select few will ever see or touch.

In all, Florida has produced an astounding 1,100 different vertebrate species that are now part of the fossil record, and new discoveries are made every year. All of these are less than 45 million years old, from the middle Eocene Epoch or younger, with the exception of fossil remains of an extinct turtle brought up by an oil drilling rig from thousands of feet deep. The nearest dinosaur fossils were found in central Alabama and Georgia.

Early drawing of prehistoric animals in Florida. Florida Archives.

Perhaps the closest Florida could come to a dinosaur was a glyptodont. Although a mammal, this creature bore an uncanny resemblance to an ankylosaurs. More than a thousand inch-thick bony plates made up its armored shell. The head and tail were heavily armored as well. Paleo Indians may have hunted glyptodonts, and the five-foot-long shells may have been useful as emergency shelters, although there is no conclusive evidence.

One glyptodont subspecies, doedicurus, sported a long tail with a ball of spikes at the end. Some scientists speculate that only the males of the species grew these deadly instruments for fighting other males. Nevertheless, I can humorously picture Paleo Indians dressed in glyptodont armor battling each other with these maze-like tails in an encounter reminiscent of medieval knights. Whether this really happened can only be left to imagination.

The major weapon of Paleo hunters during the Pleistocene Epoch was a spear-throwing device known as an atlatl. This was a short wood shaft with an animal tooth or a piece of bone, antler, or stone attached to one end so the spear could be inserted. The atlatl gave early hunters more power and range to hurl spears at thick-hided animals, such as mastodon. The bow and arrow had not yet emerged on the scene.

Most of the animal species found in Wakulla's caves flourished during a time when much of Florida was dry prairie. The climate was believed to be cooler in summer and warmer in winter. Dust storms may have been commonplace since researchers found abundant quantities of dirt that had blown in from western parts of the continent. And since more of the planet's water was locked up in ice, the lower sea levels and water table meant that Florida's landmass was almost twice its current size.

Many of the large Pleistocene animals died off when Florida's climate became more erratic and sea levels rose dramatically. It's possible that diseases may have struck them down, too. Or maybe they were simply hunted to extinction by Paleo Indians, a theory known as "the Pleistocene overkill."

During the Pleistocene era, the low water table likely made it easier for Paleo hunters. Artesian springs such as Wakulla may not have been flowing out to form rivers as they do today; Wakulla was likely a deep sinkhole connected to an extensive underwater cave system. Animals would have had to venture down into a dry cave mouth for water. Some slipped and drowned, while others may have been easy prey for predators, predators that included man.

In 1995, archeologist Calvin Jones uncovered a large flint knife near the present-day Wakulla Springs Lodge that is believed to be about 12,000 years old. It may have been used to carve mastodon steaks. In the nearby Wacissa River, a fragment of a projectile point was found embedded in the skull of an extinct bison that was more than 11,000 years old. In Sarasota County's Little Salt Springs, a wooden stake carbon-dated to be around 12,000 years old was found embedded in the shell of an extinct tortoise species.

Some of Florida's oldest human artifacts have been found at Wakulla Springs. This 2008 archeological dig was sponsored by the National Geographic Society.

It's obvious that Pleistocene watering holes were also Paleo kill sites.

Inside Wakulla's caves, too, are possibly vestiges of species that hung on for a few thousand more years since the thawing of the last ice age, but clearly became extinct as a result of man's influences. These would include birds such as the passenger pigeon and Carolina parakeet, birds that were once so common that their numbers blackened the skies. Both disappeared by the 1920s, primarily because of shooting and poisoning by farmers. Perhaps the remains of ivory-bill woodpeckers are found in the caves as well; the species' current status unknown.

Eastern bison once hung on in Florida until the early 1800s. Red wolves survived until the 1920s before becoming extinct in the Florida wild, although a small population was reintroduced to St. Vincent Island in the Florida Panhandle so they could be trained to survive in the wild and later released in North Carolina.

And then there are the lesser-known Florida species that became extinct even in the past thirty years. These include the dusky seaside sparrow. Once thriving around the marshes of the St. Johns River and Merritt Island, the bird began to die out when DDT was sprayed on the wetlands for mosquito control, beginning in 1940. Drainage was also a contributing factor. The dusky seaside sparrow was declared extinct in 1990.

What is heartening is to realize that at least some of the species represented in Wakulla's dark reaches are still alive today. These include a dazzling array of freshwater turtles, fish, snakes, and birds along with deer, otter, beaver, black bear, panther, and manatee. Some species have been able to adapt to climate changes and the emergence of a highly intelligent predator that is also capable of manipulating habitat—human beings—while other species sit precariously close to the abyss of extinction and can recover only with massive human intervention.

In more recent years, vestiges of modern civilization have showed up in the springs. The water is murkier for more days out of the year, mainly because of urban runoff entering the groundwater from points north.

In 1997, a nonnative aquatic plant first appeared—hydrilla. Originally imported from India for the aquarium trade, the invasive plant spread and grew at alarming rates, smothering Wakulla's native plants and clogging the river. Increased nitrogen flowing from the springs helped to create a two-headed hydra: it served as liquid fertilizer for hydrilla, boosting its phenomenal growth rate, and it also prompted growth of ugly brown algae that coated underwater rock formations.

Herbicide applications and hand-clearing projects attempt to keep hydrilla at bay, but the rise in nitrates is a sticky problem. Cumulative effects of runoff, septic tanks, and Tallahassee sewage sprayfields keep escalating. Even rainwater contributes some nitrates, mostly from coal-fired power plants in Alabama and Georgia.

Wakulla and many other springs are similar to the painting of

Dorian Gray. They take on our waste—what we flush down our toilets and what drains off our roads and yards—so we can maintain a clean antiseptic appearance. The more our population grows and the more we look the other way, the uglier the natural canvas of Wakulla Springs becomes. "Springs die a slow death of a thousand wounds," said Jim Stevenson, former chairman of the Florida Springs Task Force.

Solutions are readily available and are being pursued by Tallahassee and outlying areas: reuse of reclaimed water on golf courses and rights-of-way; better treatment and filtration of pollution; regular maintenance of septic tanks; more sensitivity in the use of fertilizers and pesticides; innovative alternatives to sprayfields such as artificial wetlands; and protecting the "springshed" from intense development. The obvious question arises—do we have the commitment and money to clean up and protect Wakulla Springs? What about the hundreds of other freshwater springs in Florida, which together might represent the largest concentration on earth? Are we serious about our stewardship responsibilities?

On most visits to Wakulla Springs, with the water increasingly murky, the immediate needs are obvious—we must act now! But Wakulla Springs also has a way of stretching out time and giving one perspective. Al Burt writes, "Whatever the distractions and distortions around them—however strip-zoned and ugly the road there might be, and however concreted and constrained those once sandy banks might have become—springs still can deliver a living piece of Florida that performs much the same way it did during our childhood, and even before that."

Perched over Wakulla's main boil with evening sun rays flickering through ancient cypress, Burt's words ring true. You can almost hear cries of mastodon and saber-tooth cat, or maybe panther, who roamed these parts only a half-second ago in terms of geologic time. It's not difficult to glimpse the flash of a brown arm hurtling a stone-tipped spear, smell wood smoke from a long ago campfire, and hear words of a forgotten tongue. Wakulla evokes such visions for these are Wakulla's whispers, still living in the incredible boil of her springs.

Perhaps our time here will one day be part of her murmur. I hope it tells the story of how we cleaned up Wakulla Springs, and helped several imperiled species survive into the distant future.

2

The Panther Trackers

No animal species symbolizes wild Florida more than the Florida panther, also known as puma, cougar, painter, catamount, mountain lion, red tiger. Elusive, sleek, and powerful, rarity adds to its mystery. Few people have seen a Florida panther in the wild, yet most will speak of it with awe, even when viewing a captive animal. I was no different.

Working for *Florida Wildlife* magazine from 2001 through 2003

Panther track in South Florida's Okaloacoochee Slough.

gave me a rare opportunity, one I didn't want to pass up since the magazine's survival was perennially threatened by budget cuts. I wanted to see a Florida panther in the wild, and write about the encounter.

In summer, I e-mailed Darrell Land, project leader for Florida's panther recovery efforts. Darrell worked for the same agency that published the magazine, the Florida Fish and Wildlife Conservation Commission (FWC). That gave me an in. Darrell seemed open to the idea of me joining the four-person panther capture team in the field, but he said that most capture work wouldn't begin until winter, when temperatures and water levels made for better tracking. I would be put on a list, he said. Then, I waited, and waited.

During the winter holidays, I called Darrell, anxious. He said that unusually high water levels were making the work difficult, but that yes, I could come down in a few days. "Wear some old boots," Darrell warned. "You'll be doing some wading. Also, bring some snacks. We don't always stop for lunch. We keep a hectic schedule this time of year as we try to take advantage of the limited cool weather."

Darrell said the team was currently searching for Panther 109. The big male was missing two-thirds of his tail. His radio collar wasn't working, and they wanted to capture the cat and replace the collar. He was last seen in a newly established 34,722-acre wildlife management area near Immokalee called the Okaloacoochee Slough, or OK Slough for short.

Then Darrell gave me the clincher: "Mark Lotz will be picking you up in front of your motel at 5:30 A.M."

Five-thirty A.M.!? I silently screamed. Are we milking cows?

"Sure, no problem," I lied.

Darrell chuckled, adding, "Welcome to the show."

I felt like journalist George Plimpton playing football for the Detroit Lions. Tracking panthers with the panther capture team was known to be highly specialized, challenging, and rigorous.

Three days later, an hour or more before dawn, I was riding shotgun in Mark Lotz's truck while traveling through the migrant farm

Panther kitten in den. Photo courtesy of FWC.

worker town of Immokalee. Already, loaded buses were heading to fields where workers would begin a grueling 12-hour day picking fruits and vegetables. The winds of fate blow people in different directions, I realized. Moaning about my lack of sleep seemed trivial.

"How do panthers negotiate through all that farm country?" I asked Mark, trying to snap my mind awake. He seemed bright-eyed and fully alert. An occasional headlight illuminated his lean frame and panther-colored hair. Few people are capable of being interviewed that early in the morning, but I had been picking his brain for the previous half-hour and he was answering my questions in clear, complete sentences. Maybe it was a common trait in panther biologists.

"We found a female who set up a den completely surrounded by tomato fields," he said, sipping coffee, "but the den was in a water retention area, so it had some native vegetation and thick cover.

I'm sure her movements were timed for when the workers weren't out there. There was enough wild area near that location where she could go over and hunt and get some food. That's what made the area work for her."

Mark explained that a typical panther den was located in a palmetto thicket; a panther does little to the area except to lie down and flatten out a spot.

Using radio telemetry, researchers monitor the mother panther over a period of time. They can pinpoint the den's location and determine when the mother panther leaves to hunt. While the mother is away, the team can quickly move in to gauge the health of the panther kittens. They also place transponders under their skin that act like tattoos, permanently marking each individual. "If we find that cat later on, we have a portable scanner that reads the transponder code and we can determine its lineage and where it came from," said Mark.

"We try to get to the den when the kittens are about two weeks old. At that age, they're still too young to go off on their own when we approach. They do put up a good show, though. They growl, which sounds more like a purr. They kind of spit at you and strike out, but they don't really have control over their muscles so they don't hit anything. They're mostly just cute at that age."

While an angry mother panther has never confronted the panther team, the team had to pack up very quickly in one instance when radio signals revealed that the mother was on her way back.

As if intuitively understanding my sudden desire to hold panther kittens, Mark reminded me that our task this week was to find Panther 109. "In den work, we keep the number of people to a minimum to prevent disturbance to the actual den site."

We turned right onto Highway 832. A sliver of orange light spanned the eastern horizon. Soon, I was standing in the gravel parking lot of OK Slough, shivering from a surprising Arctic cold front as I was introduced to the panther capture team's other members: panther biologist Dave Shindle, the team leader; veterinarian Mark Cunningham; and houndsman Roy McBride. Darrell Land would be up in a plane that day tracking radio-collared panthers from the air, a three-day-a-week routine.

The ground team discussed their plan. When there was enough light, each member would split up and track in different sections. McBride would be riding in the swamp buggy with his hounds and release them if he found fresh signs of Panther 109. Besides having a bobtail, Panther 109 had a distinct track; a toe on his left front paw was upraised, possibly from a break. McBride had seen his tracks on a scouting mission over the weekend. Since the dogs would chase any cat, and other panthers and several bobcats roamed the area, McBride wanted them to focus solely on Panther 109. That meant finding a fresh sign.

"In the morning, the scent is stronger," said McBride, explaining the early gathering time. "It dissipates as the day gets warmer. Plus, if we capture a panther in the heat of the day and tranquilize it, it may have trouble ventilating heat."

The gray-haired McBride has been tracking big cats with dogs since he was a teenager growing up in West Texas. "I lived in an area where people were trying to raise sheep, and mountain lions were killing them, so there was a demand for catching them. I had a choice of doing that or working on a ranch as a cowboy. I liked hunting better. That's how I got started. I just learned it on my own, which is not the best way. It takes too long. Originally, I just did nuisance animal control, but I later got to do it for these researchers."

In 1972, McBride was hired by the World Wildlife Fund to find clear signs of Florida panthers. The big cats were feared to be extinct. He found several panthers in southwest Florida's Fakahatchee Strand. In 1981, the Florida Game and Fresh Water Fish Commission (now FWC) hired him to see if Florida panthers could be captured and fitted with radio collars. They caught a panther in Fakahatchee on the first day, and another one nine days later. The cats were fitted with radio collars and released.

McBride has worked on panther captures ever since. He has also helped to capture snow leopards, jaguars, jaguarundis, ocelots, and

Canadian lynx in different parts of the world, all for research purposes. "This is a lot more interesting than shooting the animal," he says. "The animal lives and you continue to learn from him, whereas with predator control, it's over when you catch him."

Sometimes McBride can lure a panther out of a thicket by giving off the cry of a wounded animal. "They're often slow in coming. They're real cautious. But sometimes they'll come," he said.

While McBride drove off in the swamp buggy, his five yelping Walker hounds riding in a pen in the back, I joined Mark Lotz in looking for tracks on an unpaved road along the management area's eastern edge. While no panthers jumped out in front of us, we spotted a deer leaping through marsh, water spraying in all directions. An otter ran alongside a pond before sliding under water. A flock of swallows burst from a bush, flew in a spiraling circle, and then returned to the same bush. While the OK Slough bears little resemblance to Tanzania's Serengeti Plain in that big cats do not languish over a kill in full view of camera-toting tourists, it does have its share of wildlife that reveal themselves, especially at dawn.

Hanging his head out of the truck window, driving slowly, Mark spotted panther tracks in the sand. We stepped out. It wasn't the tracks of Panther 109, he quickly determined. It was from an uncollared cat he called "Half Foot" because one paw was missing part of the back heel. We crouched down. This would be my first lesson in Panther Tracking 101. Mark showed me how the front feet are rounder-looking and that the back feet are more elongated. Also, the four toes visible in a track are arranged like human fingers. The "middle" toe is comparable to our middle finger and extends beyond the others. (The "thumb" is higher up on the foot and does not leave an impression.) If there is one toe to the right and two toes to the left of the leading toe, then that is a left foot. The reverse is true for a right foot.

When determining a track's age, Mark looks for leaves, pine needles, and other debris that may have fallen into the track. Older tracks can also contain spider webs and rain dimples. Their edges won't be as sharp. A subtler clue is the color inside the track as opposed to the ground surrounding it. When fresh, the color will appear darker or damper inside the track. As the track ages, it will look the same inside and outside. Condensation in a track can reveal if it was put down early in the night or early in the morning. "The dogs are the ultimate test as to how fresh something is," he said. "If you think something is really fresh and they can't smell it, that gives you an idea of how far off you were."

Besides panther tracks, Mark and I found tracks of raccoon, deer, otter, rabbit, alligator, bobcat, and wild pig, although no sign of the Florida black bear for whom this area also offers refuge. "This place is crawling with hogs," said Mark. "Hogs probably make up 90 percent of the panthers' diet in here. The panthers seem fatter here than in other areas."

We repeated the tracking routine over the next couple of days—breaking up and looking for fresh signs of Panther 109. It was a bit like the proverbial needle in a haystack search, I surmised. We were looking for a specific panther with no active radio collar. And it was a male. Males can range over 150 to 450 square miles, while females require a much smaller range, usually 60 to 100 square miles. Panthers are elusive, camouflaged, mostly nocturnal, and solitary, and unless they are seen wading across a freshwater marsh or pond, they have plenty of hardwood hammocks and palmetto thickets in which to hide.

Another reason so few people actually see a Florida panther in the wild is that they are rare. While their numbers have been steadily rising since the release of eight female Texas pumas in 1995 to help strengthen the gene pool (Texas pumas are the Florida panthers' closest relative since their ranges historically overlapped), panther numbers hover around a hundred—not exactly on par with, say, love bugs or gray squirrels. Their numbers are unlikely to rise much higher in their South Florida enclave due to habitat restrictions. Combine that with the panthers' shy nature, and it's no wonder few people see them, even seasoned panther trackers.

The FWC panther capture team examines panther number 149 in 2007 while the large cat is tranquilized. From left to right are Mark Cunningham, Dave Onorato, Mark Lotz and John Bensen. Photo courtesy of FWC.

"I've never seen one without cheating (using radio telemetry or dogs)," said Mark, who has been with the team since 1994. Before that, he worked at the Florida Panther National Wildlife Refuge on the fire crew. "To capture a panther like this one, you can't stop. You have to work every single day. You have to try to figure out where he is going and catch up to him. We will get this cat; it's just a matter of time."

If Panther 109 is chased up a tree by the dogs, which is the likely result if the dogs catch a fresh scent, the team will go into high gear. They will set up a net and an inflatable crash bag beneath the tree to help break the fall once the panther is shot with a tranquilizer dart. If the panther gets hung up in branches and does not fall on its own, it is up to Mark Lotz to strap on climbing spikes and go up after him. He will then slip a rope around the panther and lower him to the ground. Vet Mark Cunningham will check the cat's vital signs and collect blood samples and other biomedical data. Immunizations and deworming medicine may be given. Complications arise if the panther hits branches or other objects during a fall, resulting in injury, or if it "jumps," meaning that it runs down one tree and up another.

Mark Lotz had one close call. A panther fell from a tree during a capture attempt, but it wasn't completely knocked out yet. "We caught him in the capture net, but he still had a lot of fight left in him," he said. "Just as we were trying to get him wrapped up in the net, his legs were flailing and he just happened to catch my calf with his back leg. The cats never try to come after you. They're more interested in trying to get away. I just happened to get my leg in the way."

Ironically, Mark is allergic to cats, but it hasn't affected his work or his home life. He and his wife have eight house cats.

Personal safety aside, Mark and the panther team are highly concerned about potential injuries to the cats during captures. Over the years, there have been deaths and broken legs. While radio telemetry has provided most of the hard data about panthers such as preferred habitats, home ranges, den locations, and behavior toward each other, the panther project is moving in a new, less intrusive direction. Mark Lotz has been conducting a DNA study of panther scats, and Dave Shindle has been monitoring panthers using motion-sensitive cameras. "We just want to maintain contact with a few key individuals and only collar panthers to answer specific questions about panthers that may still be unanswered, as opposed to collaring every panther that we find," said Mark.

By midweek, with no new sign of Panther 109, the capture team received an urgent call from Darrell Land in the plane. Panther 67, a female, appeared to be dead. Her radio collar was putting out a mortality signal, which meant that it was giving off two beats per second rather than the usual one beat per second. Seven months before, the team had counted three kittens in her den. Land also reported that Panther 65, a large male and very much alive, was staying close to her.

After receiving permission to enter a private ranch where Land located Panther 67 and Panther 65, we drove as far as we could down unpaved roads, then continued on foot. This was where the wading came in that Land had warned me about. We traversed a knee-deep cypress dome and a swollen expanse of freshwater marsh before coming to a palmetto thicket. The signals grew stronger. After an intense search, we found Panther 67. She was indeed dead, likely killed the night before, the team concluded. She had bite marks on two legs, but the cause of death was apparently from four canine teeth that had penetrated her skull. Since Panther 65 was the only adult in the vicinity, he was most likely the culprit, and he remained about a hundred feet away, according to radio signals.

Unless a carcass of a recent kill was found nearby, one that could cause a fight, Mark surmised that the male sought to kill the female's kittens in order to sire her next group of offspring. The mother defended her cubs with her life. "When the males fight, especially if it was more of an even match, there would be a lot more injuries to the dead one," said Mark, crouching down to examine the dead panther, "a lot of scratches and bite marks on the legs and sides of the body. And a lot of times, if they're on their backs, they will kick with their back legs to fight off an attacker. We'll often see back toenails split and there will actually be hair in there. All of her claws are pretty intact. She probably managed to back away and avoid death for a little while, but once he grabbed her head, it was all over at that point."

The dead female weighed about 80 pounds. The male was 148 pounds at his last capture. While the team spread out to look for tracks, I remained with the panther carcass. Was there such a thing as a panther ghost? I wondered. Occasionally, the dance of shadows on her tan fur played tricks with my eyes. I thought she was breathing. I wasn't used to keeping vigil with an animal that wasn't breathing.

I tried to imagine the screams and posturing of the fight. Scrambling for position. Tan bodies crashing into palmetto and brush. Lightning quick thrusts of razor-sharp claws. The fatal bite to the head.

Like a house-cat fight, only tenfold.

The fatal confrontation was a natural occurrence, one that has taken place in wild country for millennia. It was primitive. Basic. Instinctual. Busy highways and ever-shrinking panther habitat are by far the greatest threats to the panther's survival, yet I felt saddened at the loss of another Florida panther, this one being the mother of cubs.

Mark soon returned and invited me to help look for Panther 65. He said he found tracks of one young panther kitten, but Panther 65 might give us clues about the fate of the other two kittens.

Following his antenna signals, we began wading through palmettos and past arching live oaks, startling a black racer as the snake sunned in a small opening.

The radio signal grew stronger.

We paused. "Sometimes, a panther will start circling to see if you are some kind of threat," Mark whispered. "He may make a move when we stop."

While Florida panthers have not been known to attack people, other than pioneer accounts from the 1800s, some western mountain lions have more recently attacked and sometimes killed humans. This fact was not far from my mind. And we had no weapons.

Drawing closer, we would move and stop, move and stop, all the while listening. Nothing. Only songbirds.

The big male panther was somewhere inside the densest palmetto thicket I had ever seen. And close. Maybe 30 or 40 feet. Maybe less. Yet, we could neither see nor hear him, or penetrate the great wall of saw-toothed blades and pointed palmetto fans. No matter how much I tried to be stealthy, I snapped twigs and rustled palmetto fronds. Panthers, on the other hand, are generally silent and swift in pursuit or flight.

Without radio telemetry, I knew our efforts would be like grade school students trying to teach trigonometry to a group of math teachers. Panthers are master hunters, and masters of hiding. Even with radio telemetry, we had to backtrack.

After Mark Cunningham removed organs from the dead female for biomedical study, the team arranged five motion-sensitive, infrared cameras around the body. If the kittens were still alive, they would likely return to their mother and be captured on film. I would later learn that one kitten was photographed, a female. She was captured and taken to a rehab facility to continue her survival training, whereupon she was released back into the wild a few months later. So, one female panther had died, but another had survived to take her place. The panther team had meddled with a natural process, one of life and death, in order to perpetuate an endangered species.

On my way home, I stopped for a hike at the Two-Mile Prairie State Forest near Ocala. Walking through the piney woods and oak hammocks, I found myself studying tracks in the sugar sand roads—only those of dogs and deer, I determined. At one point, I gazed into a palmetto thicket, one canopied by arching live oaks. Perfect cover for panthers, I thought. Yet, I knew there were no panthers. Something was missing; a key element of the food chain had been removed as it had throughout the Southeast. While cars and trucks whined unceasingly in the distance, I felt a sudden sense of loss.

Panther withdrawal.

I consoled myself in knowing that panthers are still living free in South Florida, and that a handful of males have stealthily moved past urban areas and through the congested east-west corridor of Interstate 4. They are shunning shopping centers and theme parks, but tolerating cows and planted pines. Golf courses and citrus groves are places to traverse quickly, subdivisions to pass through at night. Riverbanks are safe corridors. Highways—hazardous.

Perhaps coyote, a crafty survivor, is leading the way. Maybe panther knows wild land again when they smell their brother, the bear.

Maybe in the Ocala National Forest, or in the undeveloped expanse from the Osceola National Forest to the Okefenokee Swamp, or where Tate's Hell merges with the Apalachicola National Forest, panther will cease roaming and settle. Something, an instinct perhaps, will tell them a place is home, suitably wild, that their ancestors' spirits stir on full moons and run with the deer.

Where there are deer, there should be panther. Predator and prey are inextricably linked. It is time for panther's return.

After 22 days of effort, Panther 109 was successfully captured. He was refitted with a radio collar and released back into the OK Slough. Less than a month later, he was killed by another male in an apparent territorial dispute.

3

Keeping Panther Populations Viable

Native Americans lived with the Florida panther for millennia. We don't know all of the stories involving encounters with the big cats, but we can largely assume that the relationship was compatible. One of their major problems, as recorded by Hernando de Soto in 1539, was keeping panthers from eating corpses in their mortuary at night. William Bartram, in his travels through Florida in the late 1700s, described panthers as "mischievous."

Generally speaking, Native Americans respected and revered the panther for its hunting prowess, and sometimes killed the cats for fur, teeth, and claws for medicine bundles—and to eat the meat—in an effort to draw spiritual power from the big cats. Panthers were closely associated with makers of medicine.

"In the first time, Creator had certain animal favorites, among them the panther—*kowa chobe*," begins the late Seminole storyteller Mary Johns in a recording made by the Tallahassee Museum in the 1990s. "The panther crawls low to Mother Earth. It comes close and snuggles up tightly so Creator could stroke panther's soft back. The Creator rewarded panther with special powers: 'your clan will have knowledge for making laws and medicines which heal.'

This is how the panther clan began and why members of the clan serve as healers and keepers of the great ceremony."

One notable case of a Native American killing a panther for medicinal purposes garnered headlines for years. The incident occurred in 1983 when Seminole leader James Billie shot a panther and claimed that it was his right as a Native American on Indian land. His defense team later argued that proof was lacking that the animal he shot was definitely a Florida panther. Billie was eventually acquitted.

After the trial, Billie, one of few humans in the twentieth century to have eaten Florida panther, was asked by a reporter, "What does panther taste like?"

"It tastes like a cross between manatee and bald eagle," Billie famously responded.

In 2004, Miccosukee tribal members became nervous when a young male panther, still dependent upon his mother, was seen several times near a ceremonial area. They alerted wildlife officials. The cat was removed to a region about 60 miles away, but within months it was killed in a turf battle with an older established male panther, underlining the challenges of relocating panthers within the current panther habitat.

Several human/panther encounters occurred in the 1800s, when the big cats were more numerous and settlers were moving into their territories. The accounts were primarily of people frightened by panther screams at night, confusing mating rituals with a portending attack. Elizabeth Cantrell, in *When Kissimmee Was Young*, wrote about her father's encounter with a panther in Kissimmee. He was walking a schoolteacher home one night when they met "the savage animal." "He says the scream of the panther is like the voice of a woman terrified beyond all imagination," she wrote, "and is enough to curdle the blood of any one who hears it, and his was no exception." According to the story, the panther advanced steadily toward them and faced them for several minutes, still screaming. Then, "by the mercy of Providence, and he can think it nothing less, the great cat slowly turned, and still screaming vanished in the darkness of the swamp."

A Miami woman in the nineteenth century reported that a panther loped after her as she rode her bicycle with a beefsteak in her basket. Near Juno in 1895, a female panther mauled two young men who had killed and were skinning her kitten.

Another attack allegedly occurred along the Hillsborough River in 1899. R. E. Smith, his wife, and young child stopped their buggy along the river to have lunch. A panther tried to attack the child, but the father interceded. According to a *Tampa Tribune* account at the time, "the cat bit Mr. Smith terribly on his arm, and, fastening its claws in his clothing, tore his coat and shirt almost completely from his body. Fortunately, Mr. Smith succeeded in getting a good grip on the animal's throat, and being a powerful man physically, he managed to maintain his hold, tightening it until he choked the cat to death." The article stated that the family proudly showed off the dead panther in Thonotosassa.

Panthers did prey on livestock on occasion, especially when deer—their primary prey animal—became scarce because of overhunting. For this reason, predators such as panthers and wolves were killed at every opportunity. In 1887, a $5 bounty was offered by the state of Florida for any panther scalp. The eradication efforts were highly successful. Panthers could be treed by dogs and then easily shot. Traps were another popular means.

Conflicts between humans and panthers quieted in the early twentieth century when panther numbers dropped significantly. The opening of the Tamiami Trail in 1927 exposed nocturnal panthers to car headlights for the first time, resulting in numerous panther deaths. At one point in the 1960s and early 1970s, panthers were thought to be extinct in the wild as a result of hunting and habitat fragmentation. But because of aggressive recovery efforts, especially with the introduction of eight female Texas pumas in 1995 to invigorate the gene pool, panther numbers rose. At the same time, urban sprawl continued to eat away at the panther's remaining South Florida habitat. In recent years, encounters with humans and their pets and livestock have risen exponentially. Panthers were being spotted within the suburban wild land interface near Naples and in small towns scattered throughout panther territory.

Panther photo taken with remote camera near animal carcass. Courtesy of Mark Lotz, FWC.

In June 2004, FP 60, an injured panther who could no longer hunt, killed several unsecured goats and emus at the Trail Lakes Campground in Ochopee. Due to his permanent injuries, the panther was placed in captivity.

Another panther, FP 79, nicknamed Don Juan because of his breeding prowess in fathering at least 30 kittens, developed a taste for livestock and pets. At age ten, he was advancing in age in terms of panther years. In January–February 2006, he feasted on turkey, chickens, a goose, a hog. and an injured dog. Despite attempts to discourage FP 79 with "averse conditioning" such as chasing it with dogs and hitting it with slingshots, Don Juan returned to kill more domestic animals. He was captured and placed in captivity.

A male panther in 2006 and early 2007 preyed upon livestock in four separate incidents in the Belle Glade area but was believed to have been killed by a vehicle on Interstate 75.

Other residents reported that panthers had killed goats, dogs, and other pets, mostly in the Naples area, although many of the claims could not be confirmed since they were reported days after the attacks. Wild (and unrestricted pet) dogs, coyotes, and bobcats can also prey upon pets and livestock, and domestic fowl attract numerous predators such as raccoons and opossums.

The rising number of panther incidents prompted the Florida Panther Outreach Working Group, a coalition of government and private organizations, to sponsor community meetings in Golden Gate Estates and Copeland/Everglades City, two communities within the current panther range that experienced problems. The meetings were well attended. The effort was to educate landowners on how to live responsibly with Florida panthers with a major emphasis on building secure pens for pets and livestock, and locking up domestic animals at night when panthers normally hunt. Defenders of Wildlife agreed to erect several pens in the area to serve as examples. The chain-link pens are generally 20 by 10 feet with a six-foot-tall wall and a covered roof. Panthers are known to leap 10 to 15 feet high, so the roof is a necessity.

"We have one to two million alligators in the state, so people are getting used to them. They expect to see alligators," said Elizabeth Fleming, Florida representative for Defenders of Wildlife. "But panthers are rare and many people don't know they're here. As time goes on, I hope people will become more accustomed to panthers and learn to live responsibly with them."

Fleming emphasized that people often mistake bobcats, domestic dogs, coyotes, feral pigs, and other animals for panthers, and that there is no such thing as a black panther. The group distributes a Florida panther identification guide.

Three agencies that manage Florida panthers—the United States Fish and Wildlife Service, the National Park Service, and the Florida Fish and Wildlife Conservation Commission (FWC)—issued in 2008 a coordinated response plan to deal with human-panther interactions. Their goal was to promote both public safety and the conservation of an endangered species. According to the report, if a panther's behavior indicates a high risk to human safety, it will be permanently removed from the population through either captivity or euthanasia.

The increasing number of panther incidents regarding people, pets, and livestock since 2002 are likely a sign that panthers, feeling the squeeze of development and competition with other panthers, are trying to expand their range. Young males have ventured to the Interstate 4 corridor in central Florida and as far north as St. Augustine in recent years, but females tend to stay close to the home range where they were raised. Wildlife agencies have wrestled with the question of relocating female panthers north of the Caloosahatchee River. First, discussions with landowners north of the river will have to be pursued, with the state or federal government offering to purchase land or conservation easements from ranch owners in order for land to remain undeveloped. One key battleground area is U.S. 17 that separates the Babcock Ranch from Myakka River State Park and Manatee County's Duette Park. These are all large tracts of public land northwest of the current panther range. The highway is the focus of development proposals as Port Charlotte's urban sprawl creeps eastward outside the Interstate 75 beltway.

In other directions, private lands and highways separate the Babcock Ranch and Fisheating Creek tracts of public lands from the Avon Park Bombing Range, Kissimmee Prairie Preserve State Park, and several wildlife management areas. If a plan is adopted to reintroduce a viable population of Florida panthers north of the Caloosahatchee, there will be a tug of war between securing potential panther habitat and accommodating Florida's growing human population. And the challenges will be formidable. Conservation planners have long proposed establishing wildlife corridors so animals can move safely from one habitat area to another, but unlike highways for human travel, corridors for a far-ranging animal such as the panther would optimally need to be several miles wide.

"Panthers can't live solely inside narrow corridors," said Darrell Land of the FWC. "They need large landscapes to establish home ranges and those home ranges need to overlap with members of the opposite sex. Corridors are important, but we cannot manage down to the minimums, leaving only enough land to walk through, instead of conserving large tracts of suitable habitat."

Wildlife underpasses along busy highways would also be important or else highway mortality will continue to be a major cause of death for panthers on the move. Additionally, former FWC panther team leader Dave Maehr suggested that a wildlife overpass be created over the wide Caloosahatchee River. "Plant it with palmettos and live oaks," he wrote in *Florida Panther*, "link it with existing forest on both sides of the river, and suddenly the envelope would open and ease the pressure within the panther habitat core." Maehr added that the key to expanding panther habitat north of the river is to work closely with private landowners, several of which he claimed would be willing participants.

How crucial is it for panthers to move north of the Caloosahatchee? For one, sea level rise by the end of this century could inundate almost a third of the panther's current South Florida range. As Darrell Land and others agree, securing habitat north of the Caloosahatchee would be the best buffer against the impacts of rising sea levels.

According to the U.S. Fish and Wildlife Service, the Florida panther would cease to be in danger of extinction, meaning that it could be downlisted to threatened status, if two viable populations of 240 adult and subadult panthers were established and maintained for at least 14 years, and suitable habitat is retained and protected for the long term. For the panther to be delisted altogether, meaning that it would be neither endangered nor threatened, at least three viable populations of 240 panthers would have to be established for 14 years, and each population must have a 95 percent probability of persisting for at least 100 years. Each population would require between 8,000 and 12,000 square miles.

To achieve this goal, panthers would need to be reintroduced into suitable areas of their previous range outside of South Florida, which historically covered the southeastern United States from Arkansas to the East Coast.

In order to test the feasibility of relocating Florida panthers to other parts of the Southeast, two experimental relocations of Texas pumas in the Suwannee River basin and Osceola Forest area in 1988 and 1993 had mixed results. Problems were primarily associated with a group of captive-raised pumas that were used in conjunction with pumas that were caught in the wild and relocated. A couple of pumas preyed on livestock, and others were shot by hunters. Some local opposition was vociferous, headed by a group called Not in My Backyard. They feared for their children, pets, and livestock. Opponents also included the Florida Farm Bureau, the American Farm Bureau, and some hunting groups. Two area legislators threatened to cut funding for the Florida Game and Freshwater Fish Commission (now FWC), and succeeded.

Proponents of the experimental reintroduction included the Florida Wildlife Federation and Florida Still Hunters Association. A 1995 poll conducted in the study area showed an 80 percent support level for the reintroduction efforts, while a statewide poll revealed a 91 percent level of support.

Wildlife biologists concluded that reintroduction is feasible, meaning that panthers could successfully establish territories and sustain themselves when reintroduced, assuming the habitat was suitable. It was learned that home ranges of females in the study were half the size of home ranges for female panthers in South Florida, likely because the North Florida habitat was more productive. A report released after the experiments emphasized the need for strong public education and outreach programs before releasing panthers into reintroduction sites.

From the lessons learned, wildlife experts, headed by the United States Fish and Wildlife Service, have been reviewing several potential reintroduction sites in the Southeast, evaluating them for size of public lands, prey base, road density, livestock density, and human population. After an extensive search, nine sites were found to be of sufficient size to support a population of up to 240 panthers. No one site was deemed optimal for all of the criteria, but the ranking was narrowed down to three main candidates: the combined area of the Okefenokee National Wildlife Refuge, Pinhook Swamp, and Osceola National Forest in southern Georgia and northern Florida; the Ozark National Forest in Arkansas; and the Felsenthal National Wildlife Refuge and surrounding environs, also in Arkansas.

Many conservationists are frustrated that no timetable has been set for a planned relocation. "It is evident that unless the agencies can demonstrate the political will to move the process forward with a scheduled plan of action, they are unlikely to accomplish the mandated task of recovery in the foreseeable future," said Steve Williams of the Florida Panther Society, based in White Springs. "The cat was listed as endangered in 1967 and we're still waiting."

Williams believes that the area north of the Caloosahatchee would be a "killing ground" for panthers due to habitat fragmentation, highways, and human population growth. "If we're serious about the long-term survival of the panther," he said, "we just need to bring cats out of South Florida. The government keeps spending money on studies and little else."

One problem is that two of the top three potential reintroduction sites are in Arkansas, and Arkansas officials are pessimistic about reintroducing the Florida panther, or eastern puma, as some call it. "Before you can move a large predator into an area you've got to have a lot of support from the public," David Goad, deputy director of the Arkansas Game and Fish Commission, told the *New York Times* in 2006. "Their hands are going to be full getting that public support, and I would almost guess it's an insurmountable problem."

Chris Belden, panther recovery coordinator with the United States Fish and Wildlife Service, basically agreed with Goad's assessment, at least for the time being. "The Service recognizes that reintroduction is critical to achieving full recovery of Florida panthers," he said. "However, due to lack of public awareness and education, panther reintroduction is in many cases not feasible at this time. The Service will work closely with state partners, nongovernmental organizations, and the public to identify suitable areas before taking any steps to reintroduce the species."

Steve Williams claims that the reason the panther isn't being reintroduced is that state and federal agencies "lack the will" to do it. "We need to emulate what they did in Yellowstone with the wolves," he said. "They're just not doing that here. We need to see the connectivity of all species and understand the balance of predator and prey. Until we learn how to live in that type of integrated system, we'll never have completely sustainable natural systems. This country has yet to honor its commitment and promise to future generations."

In 1982, the panther was designated Florida's official animal after an overwhelming vote by students throughout the state, and the big cats continue to enjoy widespread public support in Florida. But a rising number of human/panther encounters will likely continue as the existing South Florida panther habitat gets hemmed in by development. Only with strong political leadership and renewed commitment will we successfully bring panthers home to other portions of their historic range.

4

The Whooping Cranes' Hopeful Comeback

Like the Florida panther, the whooping crane became endangered in the early 1900s as a result of habitat loss and wanton killing. But unlike the panther, which was able to escape deep into the Everglades like the early Seminoles, Florida's tallest bird became extinct in the Florida wild, until farsighted conservationists initiated its return.

Steve Nesbitt, biologist with the Florida Fish and Wildlife Conservation Commission (FWC) since 1971, has been with the project to reintroduce whooping cranes in Florida since its inception. To say that whooping crane biology is in Steve's blood is a bit of an understatement. Ira Gabrielson, Steve's grandfather, was a professional ornithologist and director of the United States Biological Survey/Fish and Wildlife Service from 1935 to 1946. He was instrumental in establishing the Aransas National Wildlife Refuge in Texas, the last wintering grounds for whooping cranes, or "whoopers," at that time. He also helped to create the Patuxent Wildlife Research Center in Maryland, currently the largest of three breeding centers for whooping cranes.

Gabrielson passed away before the reintroduction project was realized, but he likely would have found great satisfaction in seeing wild whoopers again in Florida, with his grandson as project director. He also would have approved of the cooperative effort among numerous government agencies, nonprofit organizations, volunteers, private landowners, and two countries—the United States and Canada. "No one, no agency, no single unit of government can protect and improve the environment," Gabrielson said in 1968 as president of the Wildlife Management Institute. "It requires the diligent attention of every segment of society."

I met with Steve one January afternoon in his small office at the FWC's Gainesville Field Office. Like many who have become passionate about a particular subject, space for pertinent books and research papers has long been filled. Printed material spilled over in stacks and heaps on the floor, desk, and shelves. Steve's demeanor seemed to reflect his office, the demeanor of a busy person. Overseeing several different conservation projects, he periodically checked his e-mail while describing the goal of establishing a viable, nonmigratory population of whooping cranes.

"We're basing this on the nonmigrating sandhill crane population," he said. "Whooper and sandhill behavior is very similar. With the sandhills, we found there is an instinctual foundation for migration, but if it is not expressed, either by migrating with their parents or with other birds, or in the case of the ultralight aircraft project, being led in a mechanical way, it goes away. It's a combination of instinct and learning. Without the learning, it doesn't manifest itself."

Nonmigratory whoopers in Florida have never been documented, only in Louisiana. Migratory flocks, however, historically wintered in the Sunshine State in large numbers until wanton killing and the drainage of their wetland nesting habitats in northern states sent the population into a tailspin. One of Florida's last wintering whoopers was shot in St. Johns County in the late 1920s. The species as a whole nearly became extinct, dropping to just 22 individuals in the winter of 1941–42. Six of those birds had been part of a nonmigratory flock in Louisiana. They soon died out. The 16 surviving whoopers, which wintered in Texas, were spending their summers in northern Alberta, far above the area where farming was feasible.

The phone rang. "Are both of you going?" Steve asked, nodding. "Uh-huh. We should take two vehicles then. We'll meet you there." Steve was making last-minute preparations for a "debrailing" of whooping cranes, a time when plastic wing restraints or "brails" on a group of young whoopers would be removed, allowing the birds to fly on their own into the Florida unknown. The debrailing would occur later in the evening on a private central Florida ranch, and I would accompany Steve. He turned to me and continued where he left off.

"Our rationale was that if nonmigratory whoopers and sandhills got along in Louisiana, they should get along in Florida," he said. "Their habitat has always been here in Florida." Ideal whooping crane habitat consists of open grassland pocked with numerous small ponds and marshes, resource-rich land currently abundant in central Florida on private ranches, in wildlife management areas, and in state parks. But for the whoopers to survive, cooperation was essential between public and private landowners and the numerous state, federal, and Canadian partners in the project.

We left Steve's cramped quarters and were soon speeding south on Interstate 75 in a teal-green four-wheel drive vehicle. With forests, grazing lands, and highway signs whizzing past, Steve described his love for ornithology. "They (birds) do everything right in front of you. If you just watch and pay attention, they'll show you everything."

Having grown up in Virginia just outside of Washington, D.C., he spent time in New York City and went to school in Texas and Oklahoma. During summer travels to wildlife refuges around the country, he was struck by the variety of land and water birds in Florida. "There's no place else that can match it," he said.

Early on, Steve realized that whoopers would fit right in with the Florida habitats he loved best—open grasslands and wetlands.

In 1993, years of planning and fieldwork paid off. A group of young whoopers arrived from breeding facilities in Wisconsin and Maryland and were soon released. For the first time in decades, the trumpeting *kerloo! ker-lee-oo!* of whooping cranes echoed across Florida skies.

Leaving the interstate, we drove down a myriad of back roads and met a group of biologists and volunteers in pickup trucks parked before a gate. Quick introductions were made, someone produced a gate key, and we drove through grasslands interspersed by wetlands and small ponds—perfect crane habitat.

Young whooping cranes awaiting debrailing (removing wing restraints) in a field near Leesburg. FWC biologist Steve Nesbitt is in the forefront.

We parked just uphill from a large pen housing six young cranes, their white and gold-speckled bodies seeming to glow in fading light. With an air of seasoned professionalism, the team quickly set up a type of outdoor animal clinic, complete with a scale. With preparations complete, six people donned thick gloves and goggles and entered the pen. The birds were anything but cooperative. Whooping cranes are big birds, the tallest in North America, and although these were juvenile cranes, they were large enough to put up a fight. The human pursuers slipped and slid in mud and marsh, as if taking cues from slapstick comedians. Eventually, they subdued their quarry, used blindfolds to keep them calm, and carried the gangly birds to a makeshift outdoor waiting room of overturned buckets.

As darkness and a January chill enfolded the group, someone cranked a generator and flipped on a bright light. One at a time, from the back of a pickup, avian veterinarian Marilyn Spalding began a thorough checkup of each young "whooper." She and her assistants weighed the birds, took fluid and fecal samples, and examined beaks, wings, and feet. All the while, cows bellowed and the whoopers' cousins, sandhill cranes, flew in by the dozens to roost in a marshy pond. The sandhills' warbling calls echoed across water and grasslands, music from a species that spans nine million years—the oldest known living bird species.

Music for the people of the crane

Judith Buhrman was one of the crane people. Working for the Florida Marine Research Institute, she has volunteered with the largely inland crane project for several years, often participating in these "avian MASH units."

"Every time something goes extinct because we've sent it before its time, it's like a library gets burned," she said, passion rising in her voice. "That's why I keep coming back, not to mention that these birds are incredible. They're beautiful, they make wonderful music, they are charismatic, and because they are charismatic, they've been the emblem of conservation in this country since 1941."

"And then there are the people who are involved with this—they are extraordinary. No big egos, no prima donnas, everyone's efforts are focused on the objective: to snatch these creatures out of extinction's way. It's amazing."

In a 1998 article she wrote for *Birdwatcher's Digest*, Buhrman described an encouraging level of cooperation from numerous private ranchers: "The landowners consider the whoopers 'their' birds, and to see these weathered, fourth- and fifth-generation Floridians deep in earnest conversation with two apple-cheeked young biologists over barbecue is to feel a rush of pure hope."

For the six whooping cranes, their reward for being subjected to a battery of medical tests was freedom. When the plastic wing

Nonmigratory adult whooping cranes near Leesburg.

restraints or brails were removed and the whoopers were returned to their open-air pen, nothing prevented them from flying out.

In the weeks and months to follow, Steve explained that the birds would gradually expand their range, strengthening their flight muscles, and likely join other juvenile whoopers in the wild. Ever wary of bobcats, alligators, and coyotes, they would feed on insects, worms, frogs, snakes, crayfish, acorns, tubers, seeds, and an occasional young bird or small mammal. The maturing whoopers would eventually pair up and, hopefully, raise young, doing their part to perpetuate the world's rarest crane species. Between 300 and 400 whooping cranes exist in the wild today.

Steve knew from the start that the project's goal of 25 nesting pairs would take years or decades to achieve. "On average, they don't usually succeed in reproducing until they're about eight years old," he said. "They make initial efforts that often don't produce anything. We're just now getting a large enough and old enough number of birds to be able to start forming good solid pair bonds that should begin showing some reproductive success."

In 2002, a major milestone was reached. A marshy pond in Leesburg was home to the first whooping crane to fledge in the Southeast since 1939, and the first ever to be fledged by parents raised in captivity and released to the wild. The bird almost didn't make it. A sibling was eaten by a bald eagle, but when the eagle returned to take the other hatchling, the crane parents thwarted the attempt. The surviving hatchling was thus named "Lucky," and when a pair of eagles swooped down near the nest a couple of months later, Lucky's parents injured one eagle so badly it had to be taken to a rehabilitation center, where it remained for two weeks.

As the eagle learned, whooping cranes are tough customers when riled. Crow and Cheyenne warriors on the Great Plains, admiring their ferocity, made whistles of crane wing bones and ritually blew on them when they rode into battle. Likewise, a Greek myth tells of cranes that constantly waged war on a tribe of pygmies. A pair of cranes will chase egrets, herons, hawks, eagles, owls, and other cranes, including their fully grown offspring from the previous year, away from their immediate nest site. Lucky fared no differently.

Nearly a year after his birth, Lucky was pushed out of the natal territory by his parents as they prepared for a new set of eggs. With an ample dose of luck, Lucky will live 25 to 30 years and sire many offspring.

Gene and Tina Tindell happened to live along the marsh where Lucky was born. If ever there was a whooping crane lottery, the Tindells seemed to have won it. By witnessing Lucky's conception, hatching, and first flight, some crane biologists claim the Tindells have seen more in the life of a wild whooper family than anyone else on earth. After the birth, the Tindells' home became "whooping crane central" for a steady troop of biologists, journalists, and bird lovers, more than 700 in all. One biologist is said to have lived on their rooftop for a month as he filmed Lucky's upbringing. Shortly after the debrailing with Steve Nesbitt, I was fortunate enough to be one of those visitors, if only for a couple of hours.

"We took down photos of our own grandkids and put up photos of Lucky," joked Gene Tindell as he and Tina toured me through their house, showing me framed photos of every stage of Lucky's young life. "When the grandkids come to visit, we have to take down the Lucky photos and put the grandkids' photos back up."

Gene is a soft-spoken retired corrections worker who chased aggressive dogs away from the cranes on more than one occasion. "It was just unreal to have something that rare come to your back yard and nest and fledge young," he said. "It was quite an experience. We've also met a lot of nice people that otherwise we wouldn't have met."

The Tindells of Leesburg reminded me of the Heiders of Janesville, Wisconsin. In 1994, the Heiders' farm was home to the first white buffalo calf born since 1933. It was seen by many Plains Indian spiritual leaders to be a fulfillment of revered prophecies, a symbol of hope, renewal, and harmony for humanity. The Heiders were inundated with Native Americans and curiosity seekers, and,

Young whooping cranes follow an ultralight to the St. Marks National Wildlife Refuge in early January 2009.

like the Tindells, they were gracious hosts. In viewing the two families—chosen by fate to be in the center of whirlwinds—it seems that something larger was at play.

Lucky, like the white buffalo named Miracle, is a symbol of hope for all species slipping into the abyss of extinction. It seems utterly amazing that captive-raised birds can pair up, build a huge platform nest together, go through an elaborate mating dance, rear chicks, tenaciously fight off predators, and teach their surviving youngster the magic of flight. All instinctual? All genetic coding? Perhaps it is a miracle.

Steve Nesbitt has since retired from the FWC. Prolonged droughts have led to high mortality and have impaired flock productivity, with few whooping crane chicks successfully fledging. "Drought is a 'double whammy' because it results in lower reproduction and lower survival," said FWC wildlife biologist Marty Folk. "Let's hope this is a short-term problem and not a sign of things to come (associated with global warming)."

Male whooping cranes are not living as long as females, with none surviving past 10 years of age. Three females have lived to be 15 years old.

And what about Lucky, the first whooping crane to fledge in the Southeast since 1939? Unfortunately, Lucky was not so lucky. When he was two-and-a-half years old, he was killed by a bobcat. Bobcats have been the main cause of whooping crane mortality, followed by alligators, power lines, lightning strikes, vehicle collisions, fungal infections, errant golf balls, and illegal shooting.

As of 2008, 30 whooping cranes and 12 breeding pairs made up the Florida nonmigratory population, and about half of these birds were using land scheduled for development. One study estimated that the cranes had no more than a 41 percent chance of achieving a self-sustaining population. For these reasons, the International Whooping Crane Recovery Team recommended that no further releases of captive-reared whooping cranes be made into the Florida nonmigratory population. The current population will continue to be monitored.

While not all well-intentioned plans to aid in the recovery of an endangered species are entirely successful, the lessons learned from the effort might help to guide similar plans for other species.

Currently, the major hope for Florida whooping cranes lies in the ongoing project by the nonprofit group Operation Migration to restore a migratory flock of cranes. Despite a setback in 2007, when 18 yearling whooping cranes drowned in a holding pen on the Chassahowitzka National Wildlife Refuge during a sudden storm, nearly 20 cranes a year are fledged in Wisconsin and guided south by ultralight aircrafts shaped like huge cranes. Since the 2007 accident, the young migrating cranes are now divided and sent to winter at two different refuges instead of one: the Chassahowitzka and St. Marks National Wildlife Refuges along Florida's Gulf Coast. By summer, the birds fly north on their own, renewing their age-old migratory cycle.

5

Searching for Bear Dens

Without saying a word, Walt McCown quietly turned to me and held his thumb and forefinger an inch apart—we were getting close.

Instantly, I stopped worrying about snakes. Instead, I was half-expecting the mother bear we were radio-tracking through thigh-deep swamp water to explode out of the dense thicket of vines in defense of her cubs. But I didn't hear any crashing noises or deep-throated grunts, only the annoying buzz of mosquitoes. I paused to watch a giant swallowtail butterfly flitting through the tangle of vines and bay trees as if oblivious to the large adult bear just ahead.

Tall, blonde biologist Elina Garrison was in the lead, patiently us-ing hand clippers to clear a narrow path through the wall of prickly smilax vines. McCown closely followed, large and bear-like himself. He raised the radio antenna and pressed the monitor against his ear to hear the low beeps coming from the bear's radio collar.

We proceeded for a minute more, and then we saw her—a blur of dark fur 20 feet away. She was gone in a second with surprisingly little noise. We sloshed forward quickly and stepped out of the water onto a slight rise. On the ground in front of us,

Bear cubs in den in the Ocala National Forest.

three tiny black bear cubs squirmed within a ring of leaves and branches that resembled a giant bird's nest. Their eyes were still closed to the world. One cub yawned, revealing a small, toothless pink mouth.

Even though mother bear could have been lurking nearby, we scooped up her cubs and carried them cradled against our chests back to the biologists and veterinarian who were waiting for us where we entered the swamp. The team went right to work, weighing and measuring each cub and conducting a physical exam, which included taking blood, hair, and tissue samples. The timetable was to have the cubs back at their den site in the swampy wilds of central Florida's Ocala National Forest within 45 minutes. Later in the day, two of the biologists would return to check on this bear family, but meanwhile the team exuded confidence. This marked the thirty-sixth time a den site has been disturbed in the name of science. Thus far, no mother bear has abandoned her cubs.

After we restored the cubs to their nursery and slogged back to the vehicles, McCown, a biologist with the Florida Fish and Wildlife Conservation Commission (FWC), talked about Florida black bears, a distinct subspecies of the American black bear, *Ursus americanus*. Florida black bears are black with a brown muzzle, and some have a white "blaze" on their chests.

"People in northern latitudes think of denning as a winter phenomenon," he said, "but denning is a behavioral adaptation to overcome periods when there's a lack of nutritional resources. Even in southern latitudes, where there's a longer growing season, bears still den, particularly pregnant females. They need to den because their young are so small when they are born—ten to twelve ounces at birth and totally helpless. The den acts as an incubator, and the mother bear basically lies there for three and a half months and grows cubs."

In mountainous states, black bear dens are often high off the ground in hollow sections of large trees, in rock crevices, or excavated into hillsides, but most black bear dens in Florida are "nest dens." Wintering bears lie on the ground, cushioned by branches and leaves, fully exposed to the elements. A handful of Florida dens are located in tree hollows or dug into the masses of roots and soil of fallen trees.

The Ocala bear study, carried out by FWC biologists and graduate students from the University of Florida's Wildlife Ecology and Conservation Department, was funded by the Florida Department of Transportation. The study gathered data on population numbers, distribution, reproduction, survival rates, and, especially, on bear crossings along State Road 40, an east-west corridor bisecting the national forest. The team captured and radio-collared more than 90 black bears, about half of which were adult females. Following the summer mating season, they tracked

The author with three young bear cubs in the Ocala National Forest.

the females to their den sites to look for cubs. In late March and early April, the work at the bear dens began.

"In the mountains, you can go right up to a den and tranquilize the female," said Thomas Eason, then the Bear Management Section leader for the FWC. "We tried that here on the first one or two dens, but the mothers were so alert, they would run off. When we did dart them, they were still getting far away from the den." The researchers feared that the mothers might not return to care for their cubs. And so, building on the work of bear researchers on the Chassahowitzka Wildlife Management Area near Weeki Wachee, where a small population of black bears barely hangs on, the Ocala team developed a protocol of waiting for the mother bear to leave on her own. "As we got more sample sites," continued Eason, "we became more comfortable knowing she wasn't going to abandon her cubs."

Following the protocol, the team takes precautions to minimize the threat of abandonment. First, researchers try to creep quietly up to a den. "We start a stopwatch when the mother leaves the den," said McCown. "If we make a lot of noise walking up there, the mother bear may disappear and it could take us ten minutes to find the den."

While researchers handle the cubs, their cries keep the mother in the area. Responding to the sounds, one mother came back to within 10 feet of the team. "She showed no signs of aggression," recalled Eason. "These bears have basically been sleeping for three months. They're groggy. They know there's some disturbance when they hear their cubs crying, and they come to check on them, but usually you never see the female."

The team hopes to find cubs that weigh at least three to five pounds—old enough for a strong maternal bond to have been established, but young enough so the cubs won't run away. Cubs of this size are outfitted with lightweight, expandable collars that fall off in about a year. Radio transmitters are equipped with a quickened "mortality signal" that switches on if a collar is dropped or a cub dies. Researchers then try to figure out what happened by examining the body and its surroundings.

A young bear growing up in the Ocala National Forest faces many perils. A hungry adult male bear may kill and consume a mother and cubs. This happened twice during the study. Male black bears in Florida confine themselves to dens more sporadically than do pregnant females. Male aggression could be symptomatic of high bear densities. With 700 to 1,000 bears, the Ocala population is the largest of Florida's six major bear enclaves. Other bear concentrations occur at Eglin Air Force Base and in Tate's Hell/Apalachicola National Forest, Osceola National Forest, St. Johns River corridor, and the Big Cypress region.

"The theory is that when you get a high density, you have more stress," said Eason. "The bears are encountering each other more often. Males are dominant—they weigh four or five hundred pounds. In early spring, there's not much food, so protein is at a premium. All those factors add up."

Highways also contribute to cub mortality. More than half of all bears killed by motorists in Florida each year occur in and around the Ocala National Forest, most of them along State Roads 40 and 19. More than 100 black bears are killed by Florida motorists each year, and usually half of those mortalities are in and around the Ocala National Forest. If young cubs escape injury while crossing a road but lose their mother, they often starve to death. With all these dangers, about half of Ocala black bear cubs never reach their first birthday.

To gauge mortality, the team disked a section of soft shoulder along State Road 40 and checked for tracks every day during the four-year study. They documented more than 2,000 bear crossings. Far from fragmenting bear habitat, the road proved to be part of the territorial ranges of several bears. Though an alarming number were killed by vehicles, this study revealed that the highway death toll amounts to about 8 percent of the study population, well within the sustainable range. In fact, indications reveal a rising Ocala population that is spilling over into the St. Johns River corridor to the east.

Eventually, some of the Ocala bears may be used to repopulate other areas of Florida, such as the Big Bend region southeast of the Aucilla River. If a wildlife corridor can be established southward to the Chassahowitzka Wildlife Management Area along the central Gulf Coast near Weeki Wachee, the Chassahowitzka's isolated population of 10 to 15 bears may be saved from extinction. "Research shows that if you move females with cubs in the winter time, the cubs act as an anchor, and the females tend to stay in the new area," said Eason. "Often, males will pass through the Big Bend, but there's nothing to keep them there. If you establish a resident group of females, the population will take off."

The Ocala bear population may be on the rise, but so is the local human population. Numerous inholdings lie within the national forest, and the border towns of Palatka, Silver Springs, Umatilla, and DeLand are all experiencing growth. Each year, the FWC receives more than 1,000 nuisance bear complaints from people living in the vicinity of the national forest. The calls range from sightings of bears ambling through neighborhoods to complaints about them scavenging garbage cans, bird feeders, outdoor grills, and compost piles, and ripping open screened porches to reach pet food.

In visiting towns bordering the Ocala National Forest, I uncovered numerous bear stories. "I moved into the area from Palm Coast a year or so ago and had no idea there were bears in this area," said Darlene, an Altoona resident. "There is a bear that lives on my property. She doesn't bother me, and I just see her once in a while at dusk."

Others sounded less tolerant, such as a man I met in a Umatilla café. "I'm sitting in my yard with my kids one afternoon and this bear comes walking by in broad daylight," he said. "That ain't right. I've got little kids. I should be able to shoot that bear."

Florida law prohibits killing black bears, which are a threatened species in the state. While there was unregulated hunting of black bears prior to 1950, black bear hunting was outlawed statewide in Florida in 1994 as the human population grew and the bear population declined. In most of Florida's bear enclaves, road kills equal the harvesting rates of other states.

The only people who track Florida black bears today are state wildlife officers who seek to trap and relocate nuisance bears. If a problem persists, a bear may be euthanized.

Mural in Umatilla on the edge of the Ocala National Forest, the heart of
Florida's black bear country.

Eason warns that relocating or killing bears are superficial solutions. "Let's say I've got all this trash and stuff and a bear's coming
in and tearing up my garbage," he said. "So, the state comes and
moves the bear away. I think my problem's fixed. But next year or
next month another bear will find that food source. Moving bears
takes away the symptoms, but it doesn't cure the underlying problem. And it gives people a false sense that this bear's living hap-
pily ever after somewhere else in the wilderness, which we really
don't have in Florida anymore. At worst, we're killing the bear. At
second worst, we're giving a potential problem to someone else."

Eason points out that a relocated bear often will encounter resident bears that may chase it out of an already claimed territory. Bears also have good homing instincts and may be killed on highways as they try to return to their home range.

The key is for wild bears to stay wild, and for their human neighbors to learn better how to coexist with them. "Many of the people moving here don't know there are bears in Florida," said Eason. "They buy vacation homes for their retirement, and suddenly they're freaking out because they have a 300-pound bear in their backyard. So, we're working hard to educate people."

Eason and other bear biologists give "bear aware" presentations to civic groups and homeowners associations. Periodically, they mail bear-related literature and videos to area residents.

In 1999, the FWC and Defenders of Wildlife—a unique public-

FWC biologist Thomas Eason answers questions at the annual Umatilla Black Bear Festival.

Woman in bear costume at the first Forgotten Coast Black Bear Festival.

private partnership—launched the first Florida Black Bear Festival in Umatilla, which bills itself as the gateway to the Ocala National Forest. The spring festival has expanded each year, and now draws as many as 10,000 people. Most of the organizing responsibilities have been turned over to the town's Chamber of Commerce. Participants are attracted to activities that include a walk-through canvas bear maze, a climbing wall, a paleontology dig, interactive exhibits, bear-related arts and crafts, and music. All are free.

Many Umatilla residents volunteer to help. "It's my duty as a native Floridian to preserve this habitat," explained a young woman named Holly. "The festival is educating people who otherwise may not know what to do if they encounter a bear." The festival emphasizes that protecting bears and their habitat also protects Florida's treasured biodiversity.

One central message is to discourage people from attracting bears by leaving out garbage or pet food overnight. "From what I've seen, the festival exhibitors are providing a lot more 'bear aware' type of information," said Carrie Sekerak of the U.S. Forest Service. "By the time participants get to my booth, they are already more bear savvy."

Challenges remain, but the education program and the Ocala bear study have contributed to easing problems. And another annual event, the Forgotten Coast Bear Festival in Carrabelle, began in 2008 to educate people about the Apalachicola population of black bears.

When I left the Ocala National Forest on the day I held three tiny bear cubs—cute beyond belief—I felt I had touched the future of wild Florida. Ocala's bears will likely continue to den successfully in the reaches of forests and swamps, just as they have for eons, sharing this place called Florida with humankind.

6

Bear Trail

This time I was alone in bear country. No biologists. No festival-goers. Just one person, and almost 25,000 acres of swamp.

About a mile in, I spotted them—tracks of a black bear. A big one. They pointed west, the same direction I was heading on the Florida Trail through Bradwell Bay, the largest of the Apalachicola National Forest's wilderness areas.

Bear tracks. I never encounter bear tracks when walking down a heavily manicured nature trail where boardwalks span any hint of water. In Bradwell Bay, one almost expects it.

The often wet and overgrown Florida Trail seems like a feeble attempt to penetrate the massive jungles of titi bushes, smilax, gallberry, dense cypress and gum forests, and hidden blackwater ponds. Except for orange blazes, a summer's growth can obscure the path. Having few visitors doesn't help. The density and often wet conditions make Bradwell Bay far down on the list of destinations for weekend strollers.

More bears use the Bradwell Bay trail than people.

For over a mile I followed bear tracks. The bear's heavy paws had mashed leaves into mud more than an inch. I looked at my

Swampy corridor of the Florida Trail through Bradwell Bay, a black bear haven in the Apalachicola National Forest.

own prints. They were half that deep. A little basic math told me that the bear ahead weighed about 400 pounds. Maybe more.

The words of bear biologist Thomas Eason returned to me: "Bears in Florida grow larger than those in the Smokies," he said. "That's because there's more food here and they can feed year-round."

Words of comfort when alone in bear country

The largest documented Florida black bear was a whopping 624 pounds—a male struck and killed by a car in Collier County—but most adult bears weigh between 150 and 400 pounds.

On a more somber occasion than a hike in a swamp, I once pulled over on Highway 98 near Alligator Point when I spotted a Florida Fish and Wildlife Conservation Commission truck parked beside an unmoving heap of black fur along the road. It was a dead black bear. I offered to help the young biologist since moving a carcass this size was too much for one person. "This must be a sad part of your job," I said, eyeing flies that buzzed the carcass. Intestines were strung several feet parallel to the highway. It was not a scene for the weak of stomach.

"It sure is," the man agreed.

"How old is he?"

"I don't know yet. We'll get a tooth sample and age him that way."

"What are you going to do with the body?"

"Drop him off in a remote area on one of our management areas, where no one goes. That is, if I can haul him into the truck. He's about two hundred pounds. I may have to pull him into the woods there." He nodded to some open piney woods. The bear would still be visible from the road, I surmised. I sighed.

"I'll help you lift him into the truck."

The man was agreeable; we hoisted the carcass into the back of his pickup. "The buzzards made him a little lighter," he concluded. I bade a silent goodbye to the bear, touching paws now lifeless. I imagined the bear scrounging for acorns, or swimming in Gulf waters. Two years before, I had seen where bears had knocked down live oak branches at Sand Beach along Apalachicola Bay. Branches and bear poop lay everywhere. It was a bear smorgasboard. This bear's feeding days were over.

"Are many bears killed on the roads around here?" I asked.

"One was killed near Lanark Village yesterday. A lot are hit near Sopchoppy, near the Aucilla, and on Highway 27 near the St. Marks River. More are getting hit all the time, and I'm afraid more will get hit because they're really on the move this time of year."

I nodded grimly. The biggest losers from our coastal development are bears and other wildlife. People can plant native food plants for birds and squirrels, but increased car traffic will kill bears. The once-remote shorelines where bears loved to congregate are no longer safe or unoccupied by humans.

I briefly lost the bear tracks in Bradwell Bay through a stand of longleaf pines, but when I entered the "big tree area," a place where virgin cypress, gum, and slash pine stand tall, I found tracks again. This time they led me to a large twin cypress tree. Where the two trunks were joined together at the base, a bear had clawed deep furrows in bark and wood, new scars over old ones. This was a territorial marker tree for a bear, a large bear, right on the trail. I felt a tinge uneasy. The claw marks were spread as wide as my own hand. This bear made its boundary clear, and I was walking along it.

As evening shadows lengthened, I stepped more cautiously. Did the bear know I was there? Did he check his boundary daily, or just every few days? I remembered advice I had heard about what to do and not to do if encountering a wild bear: don't display prey behavior like running; make lots of noise; give the bear plenty of room to maneuver. Most of all—don't show fear.

Easier said when not face-to-face with a 500-pound bruin.

Almost relieved, I lost the bear trail again. I became immersed in the beauty and majesty of a virgin forest. Delicate shafts of light slanted through the thick overstory, highlighting bright green moss that had wrapped around swollen buttresses of immense trees—a parade of green-skirted giants. Dragonflies flitted in air. Unseen birds sang from high above.

Two national co-champion Ogeechee tupelo trees survive in Bradwell Bay, well off the Florida Trail. I found them once while wandering through a tupelo gum stand. They are immense giants, like swamp redwoods, with huge burls that would make ideal perches for gnomes. The area boasted the state record slash pine before it was struck by lightning. A state record pond cypress was discovered in 1983, but, not surprisingly, researchers could not locate the tree again to update verification. Could this area also boast a record-sized black bear?

I helped volunteers blaze part of the Florida Trail through Bradwell Bay in the mid-to-late 1970s, the days before satellite-fed global positioning systems. We used a compass and lots of red flagging, and we never walked out of earshot of another person. It is that easy to get lost.

The fact that the trail we helped to blaze ended up as a bear's territorial boundary seems appropriate. Bradwell Bay belongs to bears as much or more as to its occasional human visitors. Its wildness is due to its wetness and near impenetrability, and the fact that it fell into the public domain in the 1930s. Early loggers were frequently bogged down and frustrated. The old tram rail lines abruptly end where the big swamp begins.

Hunters poke into Bradwell Bay on occasion, but they are ever wary. The area is named for an early hunter named Bradwell who wandered lost for several days in the thicket before making his way out, tired but alive, or so the story goes. He abandoned his shotgun in the crook of a tree so he wouldn't have to carry it. No one ever found the old gun. Swamps have a way of absorbing lost items.

The second part of the swamp's name comes from a little-known definition for bay: "a broad stretch of low land between hills." There are no hills on either side of Bradwell Bay, just higher ground. A change of a few feet—or inches—in this country can

Co-champion Ogeechee tupelo tree in the Bradwell Bay Wilderness Area.

have profound effects on vegetation and whether a place is wet or dry. Topographically, Bradwell Bay has been described as a huge, irregularly shaped saucer, one that easily holds water.

At one time, Bradwell Bay was part of an ancient shoreline, perhaps a saltwater bay. Beneath the dense vegetation are layer upon layer of sand, clay, and limestone that were deposited or created by ancient seas.

While tramping through the primeval swamp, one generally doesn't think of ancient seas or planetary evolution. There are too many thoughts of how best to navigate the terrain. Too many thoughts of bear.

The swamp itself is a metaphor for struggle. Countless vines weave death grips around trees. Plants and saplings fight to close openings made by fallen giants. Shadows seem to devour sunlight. Everything in Bradwell Bay looks to be choking, swallowing, or crowding something else. Even the human's path through the swamp is made at the expense of something else—carved with a machete. At times, man truly seems like an intruder. Yet, this is where we can best find our wild cousins, the bear. Take away their habitat, and they feed on our garbage. Protect forest expanses and wild tangles of jungle, and bears can truly be bears.

By hiking the bear trail, we can find something basic and primordial in ourselves. Common roots. Balance can follow, balance between our instinctual selves and the part that seeks to control nature, and one another. Bear can teach us. Bear is part of us.

I once tracked an escaped zoo bear through a wooded area near Tallahassee, a far different environment and circumstance than following a wild bear through Bradwell Bay. I was working for a nature and historic center called the Tallahassee Museum. Most of my job involved overseeing the summer camp and showing nonvenomous snakes to squirmy kids. I was sitting in the picnic area eating lunch when an urgent call came over the walkie-talkie—"Code Zebra." That meant an escaped animal, a BIG animal like a bear or panther. In this case, it was Castor, then a three-year-old black bear.

I ran down to the large bear enclosure. Standing on a high boardwalk overlooking the fenced area was museum director Russell Daws and head animal curator Mike Jones. Both bore worried looks as they gazed across a wide black water slough that adjoined the bear fence. "A visitor spotted Castor lift up the fence and swim underneath it," said Mike. "Someone needs to swim across that slough, see where he came out, and find him."

Both Mike and Russell fixed their gaze on me. I was wearing shorts, tennis shoes and a t-shirt. Russell was spiffed out in his usual suit and tie, and Mike wore long pants and big leather shoes. I sighed. This fell under the "other duties as required" part of my job description.

I entrusted Russell with my wallet, while Mike held my walkie-talkie so I could climb down the fence. "When you find him, tell us where he's heading so we can head him off," said Mike. "We've got to get him before he crosses the highway and enters the big part of the national forest." On the other side of the slough was a thick area of swamp and pine forest. Depending on which way he wandered, Castor would eventually cross a highway and enter either an airport, a sewage plant, or more than half a million acres of the Apalachicola National Forest.

"Okay," I said hesitantly as I reached swampy ground and sank into odorous muck. "I'll let you know if I find him." Mike dropped me the walkie-talkie. Scanning the 50-foot span of black water, I tried to tell myself that if Castor could cross, I could.

"Look for a big wet spot on the bank," said Mike reassuringly. "That way you can tell where he came out and you might be able to track him from there." His words reminded me of a peewee football coach sending in a puny benchwarmer to face a kid with a premature hormonal surge.

I gulped and nodded, taking my first brave step into the slough. The water was cool, but it felt downright frigid once I waded in past my privates. When I reached the middle, with water neck high and my arm holding the walkie-talkie over my head, I didn't feel so brave. To add to my distress, I spotted a large black snake stretched out on the bank ahead of me. All of the myths I had heard growing up of water moccasins biting unsuspecting swimmers underwater flooded back to me. I was eye level with the reptile—not a comfortable feeling.

As I slowly rose out of the water, the harmless black racer crawled away. Relieved, I scoured the shoreline for signs of Castor's emergence. True to Mike's suggestion, I soon found a wet spot about four feet wide and fifteen feet long. Castor's thick fur could hold a lot of water! I found sporadic tracks as I followed the bear's trail in a southeasterly direction. It wasn't long before I spotted him. The big male was ripping open a rotten log and eating beetles and other insects. Black bears are omnivores. Most of their diet consists of plant material. The next highest category is insects, while only a small percentage is meat. This knowledge gave me some comfort.

Castor had once been a wild bear, and I admired his ability to scrounge for wild food so soon after his escape. Watching him forage, a part of me suddenly wanted to assist in his freedom quest. I could yell at him, shake a stick, and chase him deep into the forest where humans would never again look upon Castor as a zoo animal. He would be a symbol of all that is wild in Florida. Maybe he would end up in Tate's Hell or the Aucilla bottomlands or the Apalachicola River floodplain—or Bradwell Bay—living the life his wild cousins still enjoy. He could forage, den, claim his own territory, mate. . . . Castor could simply live as a bear.

Then, like an unwelcome intrusion, the logical part of my mind kicked in. Castor could no more live like a wild bear than I could exist as a hunter-gatherer. He came to the museum because he was a dumpster bear. Castor's ability to sniff out and feed on human garbage was irresistible to him. He had been relocated deep into the wilds on several occasions, only to return to his old haunts.

There are no Dumpster Anonymous groups for bears. If you can't kick the habit on your own or through relocation, the choice is either death, or life as a zoo animal. So, Castor was brought to the museum.

From the beginning, it was clear that Castor was no ordinary zoo bear. I once spotted him high in a tree feeding on tent caterpillars. He liked to swim, roll over logs, and bat around a tire hung for him as a toy. As far as a zoo environment goes, the museum had a roomy, natural-looking enclosure with shade, water, plenty of trees, and bugs. Still, it was not the wild; it was not freedom.

I radioed Mike that I had found Castor, betraying my position and my previous notion of aiding and abetting a fugitive. Castor lifted his head and snorted at me. At that point, it struck me as a bit funny that I was tracking a semi-wild black bear while armed with a walkie-talkie. The trees around me were short and spindly, difficult for a human to climb but easy for a black bear.

A black bear can climb a 100-foot tree in 30 seconds, a bear biologist had told me. "If you climb a tree to get away from a bear, he'll meet you at the top," she said. Running would only trigger an animal's chase instinct, so if Castor became aggressive, I would put up a weak defense. If he was in a playful mood, I would turn out to be a fragile playmate. Fortunately, Castor ran in the opposite direction. I followed at a safe distance. Florida black bears have never attacked a human—that we know of. Perhaps they just never found the bodies. . . .

The next hour was spent in a cat and mouse game with me finding Castor, relaying his position to those trying to head him off, and chasing him as he ran from me. Finally, dripping with sweat and still soggy from the slough, I spotted Mike and other animal keepers ahead on a dirt road. As Castor ran by them, Mike shot a tranquilizer dart in his rear. It was only a matter of minutes before we found the panting animal lying on his side, eyes open. Cautiously, we moved forward. Large paws were unmoving, paws that would never again touch wild earth. In silence, we began the

Castor, a nuisance bear now housed at the Tallahassee Museum.

laborious process of rolling Castor onto a tarp and dragging him to the road.

In hiking through Bradwell Bay, with darkness closing in and knowing I had two or more miles to go before reaching a road, I focused on getting out. Just as I left the big tree area, I spotted bear tracks again. This time the bear had only briefly followed the trail before veering north, back toward the heart of the swamp.

Female black bears require 10 to 15 square miles of wild territory; males require four to five times that amount. Since scores of bears are killed each year while crossing busy highways, big roadless areas like Bradwell Bay are crucial to their survival. And if a bear wants to use an orange-blazed hiking trail for a territorial boundary, I won't argue with him. You kind of expect that in a place like Bradwell Bay.

Return of the Ivory-bill?

The first sound I heard after launching my kayak in Holmes Creek was a loud rapping of a woodpecker in the floodplain forest across the channel. Ivory-bill? I paddled closer, seeking a glimpse of North America's largest and rarest woodpecker, believed to be extinct for more than half a century until an ivory-bill was identified by ornithologists in Arkansas' Big Woods in 2004. That sighting was closely followed by reports that ivory-bills still survived in the Choctawhatchee River Basin of the Florida Panhandle, of which Holmes Creek is a part.

Hugging the shore, I spotted a large shadowy woodpecker flying beneath a cypress canopy. I still wasn't sure of its identity, so I paddled downstream in the direction of the flying bird. Then I heard it—a familiar rising laugh-like call. Clearly, a common pileated woodpecker, North America's second largest woodpecker and native to several different habitat types—even my backyard. Oh, well. I didn't think I'd be that lucky in the first few minutes of paddling, but I found myself searching the treetops more than usual.

Ivory-billed woodpeckers are about 20 inches long, weighing more than a pound. Their wingspan is an impressive 31 inches.

Large cypress trees along North Florida's Holmes Creek, a possible refuge of the ivory-billed woodpecker.

Ivory-billed woodpecker drawing. Courtesy of Florida Archives.

Their size alone prompted some early observers to exclaim "Lord God what a bird!" or "Lord God what a woodpecker!," one reason the ivory-bill has been called "The Lord God Bird." The ivory-bill's markings are also captivating. Two white stripes extend from its head down the back to large white wing patches. The rest of its body is a deep black except for a red crest on the male birds.

Ivory-bill expert Jerome Jackson best describes the unique characteristics of the ivory-bill in his book *In Search of the Ivory-Billed Woodpecker*. In a museum, he examined two stuffed specimens side by side, one a pileated and the other an ivory-bill.

> By itself, the pileated was impressive; next to the ivory-bill, it was puny. It was not that the body of the ivory-bill was so much larger than that of the pileated, but rather that the bill of the ivory-bill was so much larger and so different. Not just lighter in color, but heavier, flattened at the tip like a carpenter's wood chisel. Its feet also seemed bigger and its claws longer and more curved, its crest longer and more pointed, its tail stiffer and with the vanes of feathers uniquely curved inward to form somewhat of a trough on the underside. I not only wanted to see the ivory-bill, I wanted to study its behavior and ecology, to understand its adaptations for existence, to understand and be able to do something about its precarious status.

John James Audubon in his *Birds of America* was a bit more poetic. Of course, he had the chance to observe ivory-bills in the wild at various locations, and he described the bird's distinctive horn-like calls and flying patterns.

> Its notes are clear, loud, and yet rather plaintive. They are heard at some considerable distance, perhaps half a mile, and resemble the false high note of a clarinet . . . pait, pait, pait. . . . The transit from one tree to another, even should the distance be as much as a hundred yards, is performed by a single sweep, and the bird appears as if merely swinging itself from the top of one tree to that of the other, forming an elegantly curved line. At this moment all the beauty of the plumage is exhibited, and strikest the beholder with pleasure. . . . I have always imagined, that in the plumage of the beautiful ivory-billed woodpecker, there is something very closely allied to the style of colouring of the great Vandyke.

Southeastern Native Americans referred to the ivory-bill as "the warrior's bird" due to its incredible power in stripping bark off dead trees to gain access to the beetles and larvae underneath. The bills of the great birds were traded and prized by Native Americans throughout the eastern United States and one bill was even found in a Colorado Native American burial, hundreds of miles from the bird's native range.

"The 'Northern Indians' . . . purchase them from the 'Southern' people at the price of two, and sometimes three buckskins a bill," wrote Mark Catesby in 1731. Tufts and bills of ivory-bills were used to decorate coronets, belts, and sacred pipes. Ivory-bill parts were often included in medicine bundles as a way for warriors to seek the ivory-bill's power in pursuing prey; they could carve up a tree like no other bird.

Even today, the "warrior's bird" is celebrated in the art of southeastern Muskogee Creek people in their finely carved shell gorgets and shell dippers. The ivory-bill is sometimes depicted as being surrounded by stars since part of the constellation Orion is a woodpecker constellation in native lore.

While Native Americans certainly had some impact on ivory-bill populations since the bird was never considered common because of their need for large ranges, nonnative collectors had a much greater impact. Audubon reported that steamboat passengers paid 25 cents for two or three ivory-bill heads. Collectors were often under the mistaken belief that the bills were made of real ivory and that they held some monetary value, often using them to decorate watch fobs. As the bird became rarer, the demand for skins and bills rose exponentially. The trade was similar to modern-day enthusiasts collecting rare coins, stamps, baseball cards, or nearly anything else perceived as "scarce," and the demand set the market price. In the 1890s, hunters along the lower Suwannee region received up to five dollars apiece for fresh specimens, the equivalent of two weeks' worth of wages for many people.

Florida, having perhaps the most concentrated and accessible ivory-bill populations, became the most popular collection site.

One man killed between 20 and 25 birds in a 10-year period in the Sanford area alone. Private collectors and museums fueled the collection craze. Museum specimens from Florida amounted to more than 150 birds. The largest numbers were taken from forested wetlands around Tampa Bay, Ft. Myers, the Ochlockonee watershed, and the lower Suwannee. But while some collectors were being richly rewarded for dead ivory-bills, people in the Big Bend's Wacissa River area were eating them. In 1895, one Wacissa hunter stated that they were "better than ducks." Also, meat from ivory-bills were likely used to bait trot lines, a practice once commonly used with pileated woodpeckers. Other birds were simply shot out of curiosity.

Habitat destruction also had a huge impact on the bird's survival. At a time when pristine tracts of the country's western landscape were being protected as part of a burgeoning national park system, the South was largely ignored. Vast swamps such as the Okefenokee and Big Cypress and the great bottomland forests along the region's alluvial rivers, with their majestic old-growth cypress and hardwood trees, were clear-cut to meet a growing demand for lumber. Ivory-bills used the large trees for nesting, and they needed vast tracts of dead and dying trees for feeding. Without them, their survival was in jeopardy.

"Greed knows no bounds," wrote Dr. Geoffrey Hill in *Ivorybill Hunters*, "and the complete consumption of the vast cypress forests (and simultaneously the long-leaf pine forests in the uplands surrounding the cypress swamps) in less than a century stands as one of the greatest feats of resource gluttony in American history."

My 1990 Florida birding guide stated that ivory-bills may have become extinct due to an "inability to adapt." That's true—failure to adapt to being shot, stuffed, eaten, and having its habitat obliterated.

While the ivory-bills were drastically declining, or believed extinct, bird lovers put forth a concerted effort to find the last remaining ivory-bills and protect them. In 1949, Audubon birdwatcher

Whitney Eastman led a search party into the Chipola River bottomlands of Calhoun County, the conclusion of a multiyear search for surviving ivory-bills. To his delight, he found two ivory-bills. Later, two more were found by the team for a total of four birds. "It was the greatest thrill of my bird-watching life when I brought that ivory-bill into my glasses," Eastman said in a 1950 *Florida Wildlife* article.

The Florida Game and Fresh Water Fish Commission, now the Florida Fish and Wildlife Conservation Commission (FWC), assisted in negotiations with timber companies in establishing a 1,300-acre wildlife preserve where the ivory-bills were seen. When no additional sightings were reported, however, sanctuary status was discontinued in 1952. One can only assume that the tract—having remained in private hands—was eventually logged.

A handful of other ivory-bill sightings by experienced bird-watchers in Florida were reported in the 1950s and 1960s. Locations included Homosassa Springs, the Aucilla River bottomlands, Eglin Air Force Base, and the Green Swamp. In the late 1960s, a feather found near a tree cavity by ivory-bill chasers northwest of Lake Okeechobee was identified as an ivory-bill's innermost secondary. In 1985, a birdwatcher reported to have watched an ivory-bill at close range for about 15 minutes along the Loxahatchee River in Jonathan Dickinson State Park.

In other parts of the South, ivory-bill sightings came in from Texas and Louisiana. Many of these claims were given little credence. James Tanner, largely regarded as the leading ivory-bill expert, believed that the ivory-bill had become extinct in the United States since the early 1940s after Louisiana's old-growth Singer Tract was logged.

After Tanner's proclamation, even noted ornithologist John Dennis, who had photographed ivory-bills in Cuba in 1948, was largely discredited when he claimed to have rediscovered the ivory-bill in the Big Thicket of East Texas in 1966. Dennis produced no photographic proof. His 1968 sound recording that he claimed were ivory-bill kent calls was ignored by his peers until years after his death. It seemed that few experts wanted to go out on the proverbial limb and become discredited by claiming to have found an extinct ivory-bill, or supporting someone else's claim.

"If the question of its existence remains unanswered," Don Moser wrote in a 1972 *Life* magazine article about the ivory-bill, "it will continue to range the back country of the mind, and those who wish to trail it there can find it in their visions."

Having explored Florida's wetlands since 1968, I've always thought of the ivory-bill in the past tense. That's because I've never seen "the Lord God bird," nor had I met anyone who claimed to have seen one during my lifetime. "My grandmother used to point out ivory-bill woodpeckers to me," my friend Andrew Ramsey told me when he learned of my interest. Ramsey has lived along North Florida's Apalachicola River for more than 80 years. "They were huge, with white stripes down their back, but I haven't seen any since I was about nine years old."

Ivory-bills were always extinct in my mind, except maybe in Cuba. They had gone the way of the passenger pigeon, Carolina parakeet, and Elvis. They lived on in stories, literature, and art. A footnote in history. End of story.

Then came a 2004 report from kayaker Gene Sparling. He claimed to have observed an ivory-bill foraging on a large cypress for more than a minute while kayaking through Bayou de View, part of the expansive Big Woods of Arkansas. Gene knew pileated woodpeckers because they nested on his farm, and this was no pileated, he said. He described his sighting as part of an online trip report for his paddling club, and it caught the attention of lifelong birding enthusiast Tim Gallagher and ivory-bill chaser Bobby Harrison. The three quickly arranged a paddling trip through the swamp. On the expedition's second day, Gene paddled on ahead in his kayak while Tim and Bobby paddled a slower canoe. In *The Grail Bird*, Gallagher describes what occurred next, a brief encounter with a wild bird that sent shock waves through the animal-loving world:

As we paddled along, we talked and joked about floating through the trackless swamp. Then Bobby started to grouse that we were being way too noisy to see any ivory-bills.

"We don't need to worry about that," I said. "The road's so loud, they'll never hear us coming. And who knows, maybe Gene will chase one back to us."

And then it happened. Less than eighty feet away, a large black-and-white bird that had been flying toward us from a side channel of the bayou to the right came out into the sunshine and flew across the open stretch of water directly in front of us. It started to bank, giving us a superb view of its back and both wings for a moment as it pulled up, as if it were going to land on a tree trunk. "Look at all the white on its wings!" I yelled. Hearing my voice, it veered away from the tree and continued to fly to the left. We both cried out simultaneously, "Ivory-bill!"

During the difficult and extensive searches that followed, sightings were reported by trained ornithologists. One noted ivory-bill skeptic, woodpecker expert Dr. Mindy LaBranche, was stunned to see a large passing woodpecker with a trailing edge of white feathers—markings of an ivory-bill, she believed. That night, while Gallagher interviewed her, he observed, "People were laughing and joking nearby, and she would occasionally laugh along with them, throwing out a comment or two. But every time she stopped talking, she would withdraw into herself. Her face at times looked almost horror-struck, almost like that of a person in shock—or perhaps like someone who has . . . well, seen a ghost."

Skeptics claim that the ivory-billed woodpecker is still extinct. That's because a conclusive photo or film footage of an ivory-bill hasn't been produced since James Tanner explored Louisiana's Singer Tract in the 1930s. A tantalizing grainy four-second video came out of the Arkansas search from a canoe-mounted camera showing what appeared to be the distinct ivory-bill underwing pattern, enough proof to prompt the United States Department of Interior to announce that the bird had miraculously returned from the grave. "It fills us with hope," said John Fitzpatrick, director of the Cornell Lab of Ornithology, in announcing the rediscovery in April 2005. "Just maybe, we did not destroy one of the most enchanted ecosystems in the world."

But had the ivory-bill survived the widespread destruction of the South's old-growth forested wetlands in the early twentieth century? Since the momentous 2005 announcement, despite thousands of hours of searching and the placement of motion-detecting remote cameras, no clear photos or videos have emerged of ivory-billed woodpeckers. It was almost as if the ivory-bill was some type of ghost bird, appearing and disappearing at will in order to torment its pursuers, however well-intentioned they were.

"The identification of the bird filmed in Arkansas in April 2004 as an ivory-billed woodpecker is best regarded as unsafe," concluded genetics researcher and birdwatcher J. Martin Collinson of the University of Aberdeen in Scotland in 2007. "The similarities between the Arkansas bird and known pileated woodpeckers suggest that it was most likely a pileated woodpecker.

"With no verified reports in the USA for over 50 years, it seemed impossible that a crow-sized black, white and red bird should have eluded the nation's ornithologists, hunters and conservationists in the heavily populated Southeastern USA for so long." Collinson went on to say that he would be happy to be proved wrong by one clear photograph.

The 2004 Arkansas claims inspired renewed efforts to find ivory-bills in other parts of the South. Ornithologist Dr. Geoff Hill of Auburn University and a small team of researchers first investigated southern Alabama's Pea River, following up on a reported sighting ten years before. They found little in the way of potential ivory-bill habitat. Since the Pea River flowed into the larger Choctawhatchee River, which wound its way through a wide floodplain to the Gulf of Mexico, they crossed into Florida to continue their search. The Choctawhatchee was little known to ornithologists, Hill said, and for some reason, rare bird col-

Large woodpecker cavities in an old cypress along Holmes Creek.

lectors around the turn of the last century had avoided the river basin.

Having poor maps of the area, the team launched their kayaks at a landing as part of an initial analysis of potential ivory-bill habitat.

Within an hour, one of Hill's research assistants, Brian Rolek, was shocked to spot an ivory-bill in flight, while Hill heard the classic "double knock" rap normally associated with ivory-bills. "We really never dreamed we'd actually find an ivory-bill," said Hill afterwards.

During subsequent studies, Hill's team claimed to have spotted ivory-bills on 13 other occasions. Numerous cavities were measured—more than 50 deemed to be fresh—that Hill claims were larger than those made by pileated woodpeckers. Stripped and scarred trees were found, presumably from ivory-bills foraging for beetle larvae by prying bark from dead tupelos, cypresses, and water oaks with their chisel-like beaks. Plus, hundreds of recordings were made of the ivory-bills' distinct kent calls and double knocks.

Many scientists and government officials view the Choctawhatchee claims with cautious optimism. "There is not enough evidence to confirm the birds' presence yet," said Ken Haddad, Florida Fish and Wildlife Conservation Commission executive director, "but the indications are promising, and we will work closely with the U.S. Fish and Wildlife Service, Auburn University, and the Northwest Florida Water Management District to see if we can confirm the reports."

In May 2008, I attended a showing of the documentary "The Lord God Bird" at the Tallahassee Film Festival. Director George Butler introduced the film, and Dr. Hill was present to answer questions about the Choctawhatchee research. Dr. Hill claimed, unequivocally, that he and his team had spotted the "Holy Grail" of birds on several occasions in the Choctawhatchee Basin. He seemed like a knowledgeable and straightforward fellow, a noted professor. And like several scientists before him, he was staking his professional reputation and credibility on the frustratingly elusive ivory-billed woodpecker.

Perusing Hill's website, I read the detailed accounts of initial sightings and viewed field sketches. One sighting was posted by research volunteer John Agnew, who was searching for the birds in a kayak in January 2008:

I heard some Pileated woodpeckers raising a ruckus about 100 yards from me, and from that direction came a large, dark woodpecker. Thinking it must be a Pileated, I wasn't in a big hurry to raise the camera up (a Nikon D80 with a 300mm lens was around my neck). The bird landed on a cypress tree about 20 yards from me, but on the other side. Thinking that I might as well practice on this "Pileated" I was raising the camera up to focus on the tree when it took off and flew right over my head at about 15 feet up. It was then that my eyes fixed on the brilliant white secondaries, the trailing edge of the wing. In the three to four seconds that the bird was in view, I could clearly see the field marks of the Ivory-bill, but still didn't believe what I was seeing. It passed over my head and off to the east. By the time I turned the kayak around, it was long gone. I paddled down to team member Sally Wolliver about a hundred yards away, and she was gesturing wildly that she had seen an Ivory Bill. We quickly determined it had to be the same bird I saw because of the direction and timing. I checked the Sibley guide with her, which has an illustration of the underside of the Pileated's wings, and then I was absolutely sure that what I had seen was NOT a Pileated! Other factors that confirmed the sighting were behavioral, the flat flight profile (not undulating like a Pileated), and no vocalization as the Pileated is prone to do. We heard the distinctive double-knock drumming sounds in the area as well. The Auburn group has had several sightings in this area, too.

Let me say that I went on this expedition as a big skeptic. I know people far more skilled than I at birding who have spent months and months in the field looking for this bird without success. I read the skeptics' websites and found them convincing, so I thought this would just be a great excuse to go kayaking in a pristine river swamp and take pictures. . . . So why didn't I get off a shot? For the same reasons that no one else has managed to do it. The glimpses are fleeting—a few seconds of fly-by in a dense swamp forest, and hesitation because of skepticism and thinking that it was a Pileated Woodpecker at first glance. I am now consumed by "if only"—if only I had been quick to prepare, I would have been focused and ready when the bird took off toward me.

Dr. Hill claims that ivory-bills hung on in the remote Choc-tawhatchee Basin because it was selectively logged in the past, never clear-cut in huge swaths, and the river and its tributaries were never dammed. And at 60 square miles, it boasts one of the largest mature swamp forests in the southeastern United States. Unlike migratory birds, ivory-bills never need to leave their remote swamp habitats and thus can live undetected by humans indefinitely, according to Hill.

Jerome Jackson, widely recognized as the world's foremost living expert on ivory-bills, was more optimistic about finding ivory-bills in Florida than in Arkansas. "Arkansas is on the fringe of what was known to be the range of the ivory-bill," said the Florida Gulf Coast University biology professor. "The heart of the ivory-bill country is in the Florida Panhandle. I would expect them to show up there."

Dr. Hill presented evidence from a search area that was roughly one mile wide and two miles long—two square miles—possibly smaller than the home range of a single ivory-bill pair, so a vast area remains to be covered. "We just need more time and a bit of luck to gather definitive proof for their existence," said Hill.

After the 2008 expedition, with several key students graduating, Hill planned to rely more on remote cameras in key locations that can be checked periodically rather than continue to launch expensive and time-consuming expeditions. "The cameras will work," he says confidently. "My only regrets concern not being more serious about keeping cameras in hand at all times early in the project. We missed many chances to photograph the birds. But I have no regrets about trying to document a rare bird in the south. I'm an ornithologist."

The good news is that most of the Choctawhatchee's floodplain is now owned by the Northwest Florida Water Management District. Logging will be minimal or nonexistent. The habitat will continue to mature and rejuvenate. Doug Barr, executive director of the Northwest Water Management District, concluded, "If the existence of these endangered/extinct birds is verified, then the acquisition, protection, and management of these lands since the mid-1980s reflect the District's intent and mission to preserve its water resources and habitats."

Still, Geoff Hill is fearful. A planned four-lane toll road and a new international airport near Panama City will likely be a stimulus for more development in the region, encroaching upon the remaining ivory-bill habitat.

"I find it ironic that the forested wetlands along the Choctawhatchee River were ignored by ornithologists through the twentieth century only to be 'discovered' as a major center of abundance for southern bottomland forest birds, including Ivory-billed Woodpeckers, just as civilization pushes into the area, rendering it less suitable for species that need space and little disturbance," he said.

During my kayak trip on Holmes Creek, I found it refreshing that no other people were on the water. What I did observe was wildlife. Alligators slid off sandy banks and turtles plopped off logs. Bright yellow prothonotary warblers flitted against shadows. Yellow-crowned night herons, ibis, egrets, and little blue herons sat poised along forested shores.

In the clear water itself, huge gar, red-horse suckers, bass, and bream darted about the deeper pools. An otter ducked under an embankment. But it was a large woodpecker darting across the channel that prompted me to look up again. It flew from a massive cypress tree. Before I could lift up my camera and peer through the zoom lens, however, it was gone, testament to the difficulty of photographing any flying woodpecker, much less an ivory-bill.

Woodpeckers rarely sit still like some wading birds. They seem to constantly be on the move. If ivory-bills truly exist in the Choctawhatchee Basin, or elsewhere in the Southeast, it may be years before a clear photograph or video emerges, if at all. The debate over their existence will likely continue. Many will adhere to the adage of astronomer Carl Sagan: "Extraordinary claims require extraordinary proof."

Still, I was hooked. A touch of mystery and intrigue—and hope—would be added to every trip I planned along a mature river forest, especially in the Choctawhatchee Basin. I vowed to have my camera ready. Since I was not a trained ornithologist, only a clear photo would suffice. Even so, I realized I was falling into a trap of chasing an elusive bird that many still claim is extinct, a bird that has robbed experts of their professional reputations for more than 60 years.

"Once we found them, what was I supposed to do?" Geoff Hill said wistfully a couple of years after his rediscovery. "The mistake," he added, "was ever looking for them."

8

The Search Continues

When I was just starting to do amateur birdwatching at age nineteen, way back in the 1970s, I had one sighting that still causes some wonder. I was canoeing through an extensive chain of lakes near Tallahassee, weaving between large buttressed cypress trees, when a large woodpecker with a light-colored bill abruptly landed on a cypress trunk before me. It perched momentarily, and I got a clear look before it flew away.

So, I took out my new bird guide, flipped to the woodpecker section, and scanned the artist's renderings of Florida's eight species of native woodpeckers (there are eight species if you count the ivory-bill). The ivory-bill image seemed to match what I had seen and I thought nothing of it, not knowing the history of the bird. When I later told an older, more experienced birdwatcher of my sighting, he smiled knowingly. "What you saw was a pileated woodpecker," he said with certainty. "The ivory-bill is extinct."

"Oh, I guess I did," I responded, not wanting to appear any more naive than I already was. Master birders can be an intimidating lot. I probably did see a pileated woodpecker. Probably. But after the Arkansas and Choctawhatchee sightings, I began to wonder, "what if?"

Dr. Geoff Hill of Auburn claims that other places in the Florida Panhandle besides the Choctawhatchee Basin might very well harbor ivory-billed woodpeckers. That's because most have never been searched by trained ornithologists, and many Panhandle areas escaped the ravages of bird collectors at the turn of the last century. He blames the late James Tanner, who many consider to be the patron saint of the ivory-billed woodpecker, for furthering the widespread belief that the ivory-bill is extinct. Hill found little fault with Tanner's field study of ivory-bills in Louisiana's Singer Tract in the 1930s, but with regard to his conclusion that the ivory-bill was doomed to extinction based upon an eight-month search of the southeastern United States, Hill writes:

> In my opinion, Tanner's attempt at a one-man inventory of all Ivory-billed Woodpeckers and ivorybill habitat in the United States was perhaps the greatest folly in the history of U.S. bird conservation. . . . His opinion on ivorybills deservedly carried great weight. If Tanner said that in 1939 we were twenty-two birds away from the end of the species, then extinction was inevitable. And once ivorybills had been pronounced extinct by the greatest ivorybill expert in the world, it became virtually impossible for the species to be resurrected. Only crackpots and kooks, after all, see extinct birds. And if the bird was gone, there was no good argument for preserving its habitat.
>
> I find it inconceivable that one person would think that he could exhaustively inventory a large portion of a continent for a secretive animal that inhabits remote swamp forests.

According to Hill, vast tracts of swamplands were missed by ivory-bill searchers of the past and present, especially in North Florida. And the average birdwatcher, says Hill, rarely ventures off roads and known areas where a wide diversity of species can be seen. To find ivory-bills, he said, you have to wade into mosquito-infested swamps—the domain of snakes and alligators—or venture forth in kayaks and canoes. Just floating down the main river channels is not enough. "Days must be spent deep in the swamp forest away from the river channel before any reasonable assessment of the presence of ivory-bills can be made," he says. "It will not surprise me if we find populations of ivory-billed woodpeckers scattered throughout the Florida Panhandle."

That gave me new encouragement. While recent surveys of the Apalachicola and Chipola rivers did not turn up signs of ivory-bills, there were still numerous swamps and tributaries to cover along the Escambia, Yellow, Conecuh, Shoal, and other rivers. Jerome Jackson found the bottomlands along the lower Wacissa and Aucilla rivers to have promising ivory-bill habitat. "All ivory-bill searchers had to do was to question the assumptions on which earlier assessments of ivory-bills were made, particularly by James Tanner, and reconsider with a more open mind where ivory-bills might have persisted," Hill concludes.

With an open mind and a Canon 400mm wildlife lens, I began my search. From past kayaking experience, I knew many North Florida river swamps were similar to the Choctawhatchee in that they were selectively logged in the 1920s and 1930s, but several large centuries-old specimens of cypress and other hardwoods that were either hollow or misshapen were spared by loggers. While one area was being logged, it would have been easy for ivory-bills to move and then return once the work was done. According to Hill, ivory-bills don't require vast tracts of thousand-year-old trees. Forests along the Gulf Coast, for example, were frequently battered by hurricanes. Along the Choctawhatchee, Hill's team had numerous sightings of ivory-bills in a forest that had been ripped by a tornado only a couple of years before. These dead and dying trees were prime feeding areas for ivory-bills. "If ivorybills required forests that grew untouched for a millennium," says Hill, "they would never have been found anywhere near the Gulf or southern Atlantic coasts."

In my search, I paddled North Florida rivers such as the Perdido, Shoal, Juniper Creek, Sopchoppy, Wacissa, Aucilla, and Chipola. Of course, I like to kayak for a variety of reasons, not just to search for rare birds, but I scanned every woodpecker that flitted about. Unlike my sighting at age nineteen of a large woodpecker that I initially thought was an ivory-bill, I felt I had studied enough old photographs, artist's renderings, and sound recordings to feel confident in differentiating an ivory-bill from a pileated woodpecker.

On my numerous trips, I paddled, watched, and listened, paddled, watched, and listened. Numerous common woodpeckers came into view, but no ivory-bills. I didn't do an exhaustive search, however. I didn't spend weeks or months immersed in these river swamps and setting up listening posts and remote cameras; I only embarked on day trips. There may very well be ivory-bills along North Florida's wild rivers. I just haven't seen any yet.

Of course, there is another species of endangered woodpecker in Florida, the existence of which is not disputed, the cardinal-sized, red-cockaded woodpecker. They were once common in the open, park-like pine forests of the Southeast, but now only one percent of their original range remains. They are unique in many respects. For one, they are the only woodpecker that drills a cavity in a living tree. They peck around the cavity so flowing sap can keep away predators such as climbing snakes. They are also a social species; a breeding pair has as many as four helpers that are usually male offspring from the previous year, proving that other species besides humans have trouble pushing their adult offspring out of the nest.

Each red-cockaded group needs about 200 acres of mature or old-growth pine forest for foraging and nesting, thus the reason they are endangered. Their numbers are rising, however, thanks to habitat enhancement measures such as prescribed burning and the planting of more longleaf pines, the creation of artificial nest cavities, and relocating birds. Red-cockaded woodpeckers are fascinating birds, though not quite as alluring as the holy grail of birds, the ivory-bill.

In order to increase my odds of finding an ivory-bill, I decided to kayak down Bruce Creek in the Choctawhatchee Basin where Dr. Hill and his team claimed to have seen and heard ivory-bills on several occasions. To reach the creek, I drove several miles

The wild Dead Lakes area along the Chipola River was once ideal habitat for the ivory-billed woodpecker.

south of Interstate 10 below a tiny town called Ponce de Leon, then veered left onto an unpaved road. Soon, I arrived at a remote launch along Bruce Creek. Not surprisingly, since it was a sweltering afternoon in mid-July, I had the place to myself. A brief thundershower had recently struck to create a steam bath atmosphere, but I didn't care. When it's July in North Florida, you often have to wait two or three months for cool weather to show itself, so it's best just to plow ahead and get used to the heat, and bring plenty of drinking water.

Sunlight dappled through a thick canopy of trees as I launched. The aroma of exposed mud along the shallow creek was almost sweet-smelling.

One of the first things I observed while paddling the small waterway toward the Choctawhatchee River was that most living things fled my presence. No matter how hard I tried to glide quietly down the red-brown stream, turtles plopped off logs well before my arrival. A pair of wood ducks erupted and flew noisily downstream. Red-shouldered hawks cried. A deer scared up, its white tail flashing against the shadowy bottomland forest. And then, while I was pulling my plastic watercraft over a log blocking the path, a noisy herd of grunting wild pigs crashed through palmettos along the shore. So much for trying to sneak up on ivory-bill woodpeckers. I might as well have been shooting off fireworks.

I froze when I heard a woodpecker hammering on a tree in the distance. Since it was July, thick foliage blocked my view, one reason ivory-bill hunters primarily search in winter after the leaves have fallen. Most floodplain trees, such as sweetgum, swamp maple, tupelo gum, and black gum, are deciduous. Plus, the water is usually higher in winter. Biting insects are taking a siesta, and resident birds, including woodpeckers, are still active. They don't hibernate, so they have to feed. I had already seen several dead snags that had been worked over by woodpeckers. Could they have been hammered by ivory-bills? I couldn't tell.

Continuing down the creek, I pulled over another log and scraped a few others until the creek widened and deepened. At this

Woodpecker tree along Bruce Creek near the Choctawhatchee River.

point, large gar splashed at my approach. More wood ducks flew up, and a great blue heron lumbered away.

Then the creek emptied into the appropriately named Roaring Cutoff. This wider waterway took a portion of the flow from the larger Choctawhatchee River, and it was really moving. Rather than battle the strong current, I headed back up Bruce Creek. I didn't mind. Framed by an unbroken hardwood forest, with no other watercraft visible and no sounds of people or machines,

Paddling Bruce Creek, a bottomlands area where ornithologists claimed to have spotted the ivory-billed woodpecker.

I felt I was in a true watery wilderness, as wild as any place in Florida. I had about as much likelihood of seeing another human as I did an ivory-bill. And I saw neither. The often-used term "primeval" came to mind in describing the place, especially with the sun dipping low and shadows lengthening. The only thing missing were alligators. I surmised that the large reptiles frequented deeper water along the Choctawhatchee River itself where there are more fish. Perhaps gators followed the fish into the floodplain during higher water periods.

The wind picked up. Treetops swayed. Tree frogs seemed to invite a distant thunderstorm to visit, calling loudly in the thick air. This place was home to many creatures, but it was not conducive to long-term human habitation. Man's presence here in the past century has mostly been marked by sudden impact—logging. Old-growth trees had been girdled and cut months later. The trunks were floated out to the river, rafted together, and guided to a sawmill. Trees closer to land were hauled out by draglines to temporary rail lines and loaded onto flatbed cars. Stumps, branches, and gashes in the remaining trees were left behind.

Perhaps more than any other place in the country, nature conceals wounds quickly in the Deep South. Most wood decomposes in a few seasons, and summer's lush growth hides the rest. Only a few weathered cypress stumps mark the logging era of earlier times.

People are often random visitors now, primarily hunting and fishing for a few hours at a time. If the numbers stay low, the system can handle the occasional sportsman.

But what if Dr. Hill's remote motion-detecting cameras do produce a clear photo of an ivory-bill? The "bird circus," as he called the clamor around the Arkansas search, would surely come to Bruce Creek and its environs. What then? Sally's Restaurant in nearby Ponce de Leon would surely see a surge, along with the Ponce de Leon Motel near I-10 and the Bruce Café to the south on Highway 20. Maybe someone will start offering ivory-bill crest-style haircuts like they did in Arkansas, and the local chainsaw artist will feature a new carved animal.

The Saturday night Bingo and the Econo Lodge in Bonifay, the largest town in the upper Choctawhatchee Basin, might see a spike in customers as well. While gun-toting hunters might complain of the sudden rise in binocular-toting "bunny huggers," some budding good ole boy entrepreneurs might start guide businesses for greenhorn visitors, or maybe offer "jungle boat tours." A kayak outfitter might even open up.

One clear photo . . . and the Holmes County Chamber of Commerce will fall in love with the ivory-billed woodpecker.

Paddling Bruce Creek as golden light filtered through the canopy, I reveled in the solitude. The evening thunderstorm bypassed the creek, and tree frogs consoled themselves with simply calling each

Large cypress along Bruce Creek.

other. Cicadas whirred, but otherwise the creek was relatively still. Even mosquitoes inexplicably died down. Spruce pine, cypress, and sweetgum stood as silent sentinels.

Reaching the landing, I stood facing the creek, quiet like the trees. Shadows closed in while a slanting sunbeam hit a distant cypress trunk, a bright glimmer of orange. If there were ivory-bills in the vast Choctawhatchee bottomlands, they seemed safe, with tens of thousands of acres of protected habitat and virtually no humans. They might never be photographed, I surmised. Maybe we continue searching for them because we refuse to believe that we killed off such a magnificent creature. Given their history with our species, they certainly deserve to remain a grail bird to haunt our dreams and visions, prompting an in-depth search of our collective conscience and a reevaluation of our relationship with other life forms. We may see them again only when they—or we— are ready.

I vowed to keep looking, if only for a glimpse.

9

Manatee Haven

When Laurilee Thompson was a child, she loved to sit on her family's dock along the Indian River Lagoon near Titusville and gently place her bare feet on the backs of grazing manatees. "They didn't seem to mind," she recalled. "Sometimes they'd nuzzle our bare feet with their soft whiskery faces. The manatees still come into that little basin now when the wind blows the seagrass in."

Manatees are Florida's gentle giants, called sea cows because they graze on voluminous amounts of sea grass and water weeds. They are often curious about people, and except for occasionally bumping a canoe or kayak and startling its occupants, they are totally harmless. Red tide and sudden cold snaps are major causes of death, but people driving high-powered boats kill scores of manatees each year. Florida has more than one million registered powerboats, and slightly more than 3,000 manatees. Through the eons of their evolution, they've never had to flee large, threatening objects swiftly moving across the surface. Now they do. If ever there was a creature that needed allies, it is the West Indian Manatee.

The 156-mile Indian River Lagoon is the primary manatee haven for Florida's East Coast. More than a third of the nation's manatee

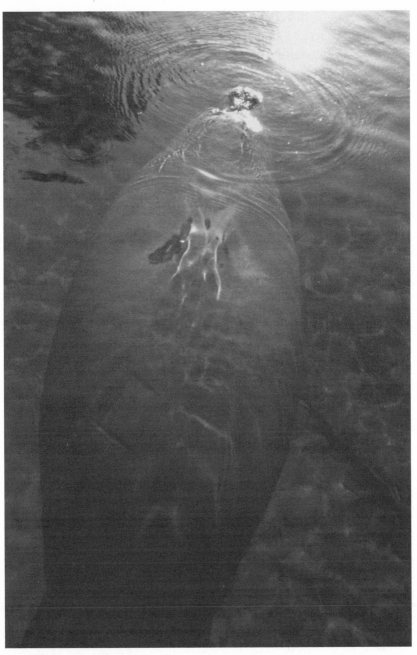

Manatee and water ripples.

population resides there along with more than 4,300 different species of plants and animals, 72 of which are endangered or threatened. This diversity is strengthened by overlapping boundaries of tropical and subtropical climates. To better understand the manatee in this region, it is important to learn about the habitat in which it lives, the people who live in and around it, and how the manatee has evolved to become an ecotourism asset.

The Indian River Lagoon is where five generations of Laurilee Thompson's family have lived and worked as fishermen and boat builders, and where Laurilee heeded the call of the sea. By the time she was 12, she had her own mullet boat and crab traps. "I was outside all the time and I just taught myself an appreciation of the outdoors," she said. "When I was going to high school, I'd fish all night and do my homework sitting in the middle of the Indian River with a light hooked to a 12-volt battery."

Eventually, Laurilee got a job on the back of a commercial fishing boat. Within six months, she was running it. She ran boats for more than ten years.

"By the time I got off the ocean," she said, "things had changed dramatically due to overfishing. With the new technology in commercial fishing, we just wiped out all of the fishing spots—it was getting harder and harder to make a living. We had to stay out longer. It was getting old." She frowned, then added with a chuckle, "I'm one of the reasons there's not many grouper left along this coast."

She was half-joking, half-serious, like the reformed alcoholic who pokes fun at his or her former self. Now, the stocky, down-to-earth woman with graying sand-colored hair and an easy smile has traded her fishing boat for a kayak, and she has become a crusader to protect and restore North America's most diverse estuary and the wildlife that resides there, including the West Indian Manatee.

When I entered Titusville's Dixie Crossroads Restaurant, which Laurilee manages for her family, she greeted me warmly and directed me to a booth. I gazed upon murals of life-sized manatees swimming and diving while several platters of broiled rock shrimp

Restaurant owner and environmental activist Laurilee Thompson of Titusville.

were brought forth. Over the years, Laurilee's family elevated rock shrimp from a discarded by-catch to a high-demand food item, chiefly because they developed their own processing facility to cut open the hard shells. While waitresses and waiters buzzed about—

this was one of Florida's busiest seafood restaurants, attracting almost half a million patrons a year—Laurilee began describing a love affair with the Indian River Lagoon. "You've got to see it," she implored. "It's incredible."

I almost didn't need to. Nearly every inside and outside wall of the multiroom restaurant was covered in colorful murals depicting the diverse life found in and around the lagoon, starting with the main dining room which was completely devoted to the manatee. The in-house and take-home menus read like conservation magazines. Even the coloring books given to waiting children depict the lagoon's fish and wildlife. This wasn't a restaurant—it was an eco-brainwashing factory!

"At first my dad thought it was a total waste of time and money," said Laurilee, referring to the murals and publications. "But when we started getting articles in *Wild Bird* and *Birdwatcher's Digest* and people were coming in and saying 'we're here because we saw your article in *Birdwatcher's Digest*,' he recognized that it is good for business."

Before I waddled out of the restaurant, having eaten more of the lobster-tasting rock shrimp in one sitting than in my entire life, Laurilee and I agreed to meet at dawn the next day for a firsthand look at the upper lagoon.

At the appointed hour, I squeezed into a slim kayak and gazed out over a mangrove-lined watery expanse in the Merritt Island National Wildlife Refuge. A bit embarrassed by the previous day's gluttony, I vowed to work off any extra weight by becoming a paddling machine for the next several hours. Abundant wildlife and Laurilee's captivating stories slowed my movements, however. There was too much to see and learn.

Although I wanted to see manatees most of all, our first point of interest was a lush green island, one of many that dot the lagoon. From a safe distance, we coasted alongside thousands of squawking herons, egrets, ibis, brown pelicans, and breathtaking roseate spoonbills. Relishing a rare opportunity to view an active bird rookery, I watched adult birds fly in and out of mangroves, either returning with food or leaving to forage. Fuzzy-headed young waited impatiently in their jumbled nests of sticks.

Sometimes, birds would spar with jabbing neck thrusts and raucous squawking. There was constant squabbling as this was a crowded neighborhood not much different than some human ones, except for the beaks, feathers, and long spindly legs. From kayaks, we could peek in and observe their not-so-private lives with no window shades to obstruct the view.

Laurilee explained that this rookery and others like it along the Indian River Lagoon were created with spoil dredged from the Intracoastal Waterway in the 1960s. Mangroves took hold, and a diverse array of birds followed. In a world where humans often cause the demise of our wildlife, especially along Florida's fast-growing East Coast, it was heartening news.

"This part of the lagoon is better now than it was ten years ago," said Laurilee. "The sea grass beds are recovering, and that's a main food source for manatees and a nursery grounds for all kinds of sea life. It's mainly due to better storm water controls, but we still have a long way to go. People need to realize that the fertilizers and pesticides on their lawns are coming into the lagoon. If they use more native vegetation, they don't need so many chemicals and they don't need to water as much."

It was just one more example of the necessary connection between personal lifestyles and environmental quality.

Laurilee would paddle awhile, then stop and describe different scenes and what it meant ecologically and to her personally. She pointed to an area north of the island that once had oysters, oysters that died off due to pollution. "We used to go there as a kid," she said. "Dad would pile us into a little john boat that had a twenty-horse motor. It would take us three to four hours to get there. We'd get a load of oysters and come back to the house after dark. Then we'd lay some tin down in a fire and pile the oysters on top. Dad would cover them with wet canvas and spray it now and then with water. Man, those were good."

Laurilee pointed to brown pelicans swimming erratically after a

Manatee coming up for air.

slicing dolphin fin. "They're following the dolphins," she said, "hop-
ing some fish would be chased their way." Occasionally, a dolphin
would flip a fish into the air and catch it, and sometimes dolphins
would pause in their search and check out the strange humans in
their kayaks.

As a highlight to this natural Disney-type trip, Laurilee guided
me up the nearby Haulover Canal to a pod of adult manatees. We
floated about 30 feet away and watched their swirls as they grazed
on lush aquatic grasses. An adult manatee can consume more than
10 percent of its body weight in a day, so eating is a big part of their
routine.

While we kept our distance from the sea cows since it is unlawful to chase or harass manatees, occasionally one of the massive creatures would separate from the pod and swim alongside us, thrusting out a whiskered snout with a whoosh of air. One nudged the front of Laurilee's kayak and gently pushed it for several feet, watching her with small button-like eyes. The gesture seemed like a caress. "They know I'm their friend," Laurilee said, smiling.

Do manatees recognize individual nonaggressive people they see over and over? I didn't have any manatees nudge my boat in that caressing manner. They didn't know me.

I was keenly aware that the manatees could easily flip us with their massive bodies and tails. They can reach 10 feet in length and weigh over 1,000 pounds, resembling a walrus minus the tusks. But they are indeed gentle giants. And they have no greater friend than Laurilee Thompson.

Several years ago, Laurilee hired an artist to paint life-sized manatees on the walls of a Dixie Crossroads dining room, the first of many murals. "I watched the reaction of my customers and how much they enjoyed it," she said, "and I thought, 'I could teach people something here.'" Today, diverse murals span more than 300 feet, a possible record for one business.

"So many people who move here have no understanding or appreciation of what a dynamic area this is," she said. "It's one of the most biodiverse areas in the world. If nobody teaches them, they'll never understand it and will never rise up to help protect it."

While Laurilee was transforming the restaurant, she had another calling. "A few years ago, the president of our Audubon chapter came through the back door of the kitchen. I was at the sink cutting lobsters. He introduced himself; I had never met him, and he said, 'I'd like for you to serve on the board.' Now, I'd been a member for years, but one of those kinds of members who never goes to a meeting. I just paid my money and read the magazine, but he said, 'I want to change the direction of the board and I think that you'd make a good candidate. I want business people on my board.'"

Laurilee, representing one of the major employers in northern Brevard County, quickly proved to be an effective environmental advocate. She linked a healthy environment with a thriving tourism industry and preached against runaway growth. Her background and nonabrasive personality soon landed her on a dozen different councils and boards of directors that promoted environmental protection and nature-based recreation. For Laurilee, it was a gargantuan leap to make in one generation—from commercial fisherman to kayaker, from intensive user to environmental activist.

Manatee eating a palm branch in the Blue Springs State Park.

The Apostle Paul in environmental garb

"What makes me kind of unique is that I've been on both sides," she said. "I've made my living for many years as a commercial fisherman, and so I can talk to fisherman; I can talk to environmentalists; I can talk to business people. I've been effective in some negotiations between these people with differing opinions simply because of my background."

In 1997, Laurilee began the Space Coast Birding and Wildlife Festival at great personal and business expense, and she rarely passes up an opportunity to show off the area's natural beauty to residents, visitors, journalists, and government officials by way of kayak, airboat, van, motor coach, horseback, and on foot. The outings are enjoyable—they give Laurilee a break from the restaurant—but she admits to having an ulterior motive. The future of her beloved Indian River Lagoon is at stake.

"Area land-use planners recently predicted that every privately owned upland habitat in watersheds of the St. Johns and Indian rivers would be completely built out in twenty years. When you really think about that scenario, you should be scared. There are other ways to have growth than to continue to spread out in this mindless sprawl."

Besides fast-moving boats that kill up to 100 manatees each year, loss of habitat is a major threat to the long-term survival of manatees. That's because rampant development, with its increases in runoff and sewage, often translates to a loss of wetlands and seagrass that manatees and numerous other creatures depend upon.

"One way to measure the character of a community is to look at what it protects—we protect what we value," said Laurilee. "For several generations my family and many others have depended on a healthy environment to make our living. The economic value of natural lands and unpolluted water through the creation of jobs in the fishing, tourism, recreation, and other industries is well documented. Corporations consistently rank quality of life as a key consideration when relocating. It was Florida's natural areas and warm climate that sustained wildlife and brought vacationers long before there were theme parks and sprawling metroplexes. When viewed merely as an economic asset, natural lands clearly pay their way."

She sighed. Both of our eyes rested on a circling manatee. The large creature seemed to be playing with us, ignoring nearby power-boats. Fear could be a driving force, I thought; I feared there weren't enough people like Laurilee Thompson.

10

Florida's Sea Turtles Hang On

The big female loggerhead turtle, seemingly oblivious to a small group of humans nearby or to the lights and sounds of Port Everglades, finished depositing about 100 leathery eggs the size of ping-pong balls in the sands of John U. Lloyd State Park near Ft. Lauderdale. Then, with her strong flippers, she began covering the egg chamber.

Since our group of nighttime observers weren't allowed to use bright lights or flash photography, we didn't see the "turtle tears" streaming from the loggerhead's eyes, something commonly seen at nesting events. The tears are a means to remove salt from a turtle's body. We could only make out the massive body of the four-foot loggerhead, her shell gleaming in the moonlight. This was a continuation of a 110-million-year cycle, and we felt honored to witness it.

Like a large ship, the turtle slowly began to turn. I scrambled out of the way, allowing the matriarch safe passage to the sea. Her tracks, the only tell-tale sign of her visit, would soon be covered by waves, rising tide, and wind-blown sand. She may return again and again to nest on the same beach during a nesting season before swimming north or south for hundreds and even thousands of miles to specific feeding areas.

Adult loggerhead turtle near Long Key in the Florida Keys. Photo by Kristy Force.

In the coming weeks, the predominant temperature of the nest would determine the sex of the hatchlings. Warmer sand produces more females. A larger number of males would hatch during cooler temperatures. Regardless, about one in a thousand baby turtles make it to adulthood. Most eggs or hatchlings will fall prey to predators such as crabs, birds, and raccoons. People still harvest turtle eggs for food, mostly in other countries. Hatchlings can become disoriented by beach lights and crawl inland instead of toward the sea, falling victim to vehicles and the elements.

Once in the Atlantic Ocean, young defenseless loggerheads embark on a five-to-10-year journey of 8,000–9,000 miles around the Sargasso Sea, often finding safety in clumps of seaweed. Developing loggerheads in the Pacific can travel more than 12,000 miles. Scientists believe that from birth loggerheads use a type of built-in navigational compass that uses the earth's magnetic field. As they grow older, they are better able to pinpoint specific geographic locations such as feeding areas and nesting beaches as they fine-tune their internal magnetic maps.

Studies revolving around other turtle species have come up with similar results. Juvenile sea turtles that are captured in a specific feeding area and released some distance away are able to travel back to the same area where they were captured. Not known are the precise magnetic features that turtles detect in specific geographic areas.

Jack Rudloe of Panacea's Gulf Specimen Marine Lab once demonstrated how the noses of hatchling turtles were magnetic. He put a hatchling turtle that died of natural causes on a fish line and placed a magnet close to its nose. Even in a shriveled-up state, the hatchling followed the magnet. This occurred because submicroscopic crystals of magnetite have been lodged in the turtle's brain and nose, helping it to guide itself like a magnetized compass needle, similar to how homing pigeons, monarch butterflies, whales, salmon, tuna, and other animals that travel long distances orient themselves with the earth's magnetic field. Even humans have traces of magnetite in their brains.

Turtles may also navigate by sensing wave direction and currents and by using their low-frequency hearing. Perhaps they can hone in to the sound of the surf on a specific beach. Visual and aromatic clues may also provide direction. Green sea turtles have been observed nuzzling the sand when first landing on a nesting beach, as if smelling the ground to ensure the right location.

The famous naturalist Archie Carr, in the 1950s, was one of the first to document the amazing migratory patterns of sea turtles. He was clued in by a story told by Nicaraguan turtle fishermen who had captured two green sea turtles. The turtles, branded with the fishermen's initials, were being taken to market in Key West when a violent storm capsized their boat near the Keys. The turtles escaped, but to the fishermen's surprise, they recaptured the same turtles some months later off the coast of Nicaragua, more than 600 miles from their accidental release site. This and other incidents prompted Carr to conclude in *The Windward Road*, "It is safe to suppose that green turtles do in fact have some sort of extra sense . . . that lets them make long, controlled journeys in trackless seas."

Did ancient North Americans have an inkling or understanding about sea turtles and magnetism? Interestingly, a scientist from Dartmouth, Dr. Vincent Malmstrom, discovered in 1975 that a pre-Olmec turtle head carving along Mexico's Pacific coast at the Izapa ceremonial center had a magnetic nose. Human stone carvings from the same time period, about 2000 BC, have magnetic belly buttons and some have magnetic temples. Scientists are puzzled as to how ancient Americans were able to magnetize the statues since no plugs of magnetic ore were found. Did they simply carve the statue around a specific location in the rock that was already magnetic?

"How a Stone Age people familiar with chipping their primary tools and weapons out of materials like flint and obsidian stumbled onto the presence of magnetic iron ore in basalt boulders remains a mystery," concluded Dr. Malmstrom in *Cycles of the Sun, Mysteries of the Moon*.

Jack Rudloe, in *Search for the Great Turtle Mother*, describes accompanying Dr. Malmstrom to Izapa and seeing the turtle head statue for the first time:

> I stepped forward clutching my compass, hoping that I would get some sort of blinding revelation that this long trek would be worthwhile after all. I held the compass steady, and when the dial stopped turning and remained fixed at 110 degrees, I slowly, steadily thrust my hand and compass forward.
>
> Suddenly the field of force gripped my compass and the needle whirled to the north, coming to rest at 60 degrees. The force was much more powerful than that of any statue we had measured so far. My hand was trembling with excitement and bewilderment, but I held it there, and when I withdrew it the dial spun back to its original position of 110 degrees. Again

and again I tried it with the same results. No matter where I moved the compass around that great stony face, the needle continuously pointed to the snout until I pulled it away. Half a meter away the magnetic field faded and the turtle's nose lost its pull.

I was more bewildered than ever. The rock could speak to my compass but not to me.

Other stone statues at Izapa were not found to be magnetic—only the turtle.

The Miskito Indians of Central America have a fascinating tale of a large rock known as the Turtle Mother, a benevolent spirit that would help to guide sea turtles and also turtle hunters, magically turning toward the direction of the turtles. But if the hunters took more than what they needed, the Turtle Mother would send the turtles deep into the ocean and out of reach and bring the hunters bad luck. So, the Turtle Mother story was a way to rein in greed among the people.

Sea turtles have long been used by humans for food. Like other peoples in the world, Native Americans stored live turtles in their large sailing dugouts or rafts to be butchered for fresh meat when needed. Eggs harvested from nests were also a food source. Stories, myths, and ritual of several native tribes honored the terrapin, perhaps as a way of acknowledging and giving thanks for that which brought them sustenance and for appeasing the Turtle Mother.

A southeastern Muskogee legend describes a time when the earth was covered with water. Turtle felt sorry for the many land creatures that were drowning. So, turtle dove beneath the water and found land, and diligently built it up to where certain creatures could survive. Different birds did their part by drying the land with their wings. The new land benefited turtle, too, for she now had a place where she could lay her eggs. To this day, some traditional Muskogean peoples perform a turtle dance to honor turtle's role in creation. The turtle is also venerated in symbology. Not only do turtle images adorn ceremonial objects and personal jewelry, the cleared ceremonial grounds of some Muskogee groups represents the first land turtle helped to build.

Along Florida's East Coast near Titusville, perhaps the purpose of the huge terrapin-shaped mound known as "Turtle Mound" was to venerate the sea turtle's role in creation. Built primarily of discarded oyster shells by Timucuan Indians from 800 AD to 1400 AD, the 50-foot vantage point that the mound afforded surely gave its builders a sense that this heap of land would never be inundated regardless of the storm surge. Unfortunately, no Timucuans remain to consult with as to the mound's true purpose, but the turtle shape gives us a clue.

When Europeans arrived and Florida's population grew, turtle meat and eggs were prized with no limits on the numbers being harvested. Nesting beaches were and continue to be impaired by development, a more permanent disturbance than the natural cycles of hurricanes and tropical storms that temporarily steal away beach sands and often create steep inclines that inhibit turtles from crawling ashore.

Turtles are mistakenly ensnared in nets and caught by hook and line. A more modern phenomenon—plastic garbage—is often mistaken for jellyfish by hungry turtles, contributing to their decline.

Boats can hit turtles as well. A visit to the animal hospital at Orlando's SeaWorld was an eye-opener for me. The shells of several sea turtles that had been hit by boats were being glued back together with a flexible material known as tegaderm. More difficult to mend were the turtles that were missing flippers due to encounters with boat propellers, or with natural predators such as sharks. It was inspiring to see people who cared about creatures such as sea turtles, and to know that strict laws now protect all of Florida's large sea turtles that are endangered—the leatherback, green, loggerhead, hawksbill, and Kemp's ridley.

The Kemp's ridley is the smallest and most endangered sea turtle in the world. Fewer than a thousand nesting females exist, and most

Sea turtle nests on busy Ft. Lauderdale beach.

of these nest on a Gulf beach in Mexico known as Rancho Nuevo. Crabs and other crustaceans make up their diet.

Leatherbacks are the largest, approaching the size of a small car. They can weigh up to 1,500 pounds and reach lengths of nearly 10 feet. They can tolerate cold water by regulating their body temperature, a rare trait among cold-blooded reptiles. This helps them dive to depths of more than 3,000 feet and swim to northern waters that could be an astounding 3,000 miles from their nesting beaches. Amazingly, they return to the same beach of their origin in order to nest. Only 30 to 60 leatherbacks nest in Florida. Jellyfish are a favorite food.

By far the most common sea turtle seen nesting in Florida is the loggerhead. Compared to the leatherback it's almost a dwarf, reaching lengths of around four feet and an average weight of 300 pounds. Its head, however, can be ten inches wide, thus the reason for its name. The loggerhead's powerful jaws can crush clams, crabs, spiny lobsters, and other armored animals, and each flipper has two claws. Florida's beaches account for about a third of the world's loggerhead nests and more than 90 percent of nests in the United States.

The hawksbill is named for its raptor-like jaws that are perfect for gathering sponges, their preferred food. Their mottled black, brown and amber shell reaches lengths of 30 inches. They tend to be found in more tropical waters such as the Florida Keys. Angelfish often follow hawksbills, opportunistically waiting until the turtles bite through the outer coverings of sponges so they can feed on the inner tissue.

The green sea turtle was once prized for its taste, especially in soup. Archie Carr wrote that clear green turtle soup "is the finest gastronomic contribution of the English people. Giving it up was my greatest sacrifice to the religion of turtle preservation." The green turtle's body is not green, however. Only its body fat, known as calipee, has a green hue since sea grasses and algae make up their largely vegetarian diet. With an average weight of 350 pounds, 100 to 1,000 green turtles nest on Florida's beaches each year.

Florida's sea turtles need a great deal of help from their friends if they are to cope with the man-made and natural changes that are bearing down upon them. And it must be an international cooperative effort since sea turtles are wide-ranging creatures, oblivious to the arbitrary boundaries we have established that divide states and countries.

What can we learn from sea turtles? Perhaps we can ponder Jack Rudloe's words after his multiyear search for the turtle mother:

Turtle Mother was no particular rock, or log, or entity, but was a spirit within the depths of our collective minds. She could take any form that suited her. She existed in the innermost reaches of my mind, as she does in the mind of all humanity, if only we allow ourselves to reach deep into our subconscious. If we tune in to the more primitive parts of our lower brains, there we'll meet her.

11

The Salamander Hunter

Famous Harvard biologist Edward O. Wilson describes Bruce Means as a top-notch scientist who has painstakingly documented his extensive studies of the eastern diamondback rattlesnake and several rare species of southeastern salamanders. But he also regards him as an adventurer who harkens back to the great explorer-naturalists of yesteryear. "His is the incarnation of an endangered species," Wilson concluded in the foreword of Means' 2008 book *Stalking the Plumed Serpent and Other Adventures in Herpetology*.

Means' explorer-naturalist resume is impressive. He has stalked the most venomous terrestrial snakes on earth in Australia for *National Geographic*, wrestled monster alligator snapping turtles in the Apalachicola River, been bitten by a diamondback rattlesnake while alone on a barrier island, and searched for rare snakes in Costa Rica during the eruption of a nearby volcano. Through it all, he has placed as much emphasis on "creepy crawly" things such as salamanders as he has on awe-inspiring reptiles and other animals. His work with salamanders in North Florida's unique bogs, pine flatwoods, and ravines is legendary. He has identified several new species of amphibians and a rare species of king snake that is only found between the Apalachicola and Ochlocknee rivers. It is part of his continuing documentation of the incredible biodiversity of Florida's Big Bend and Panhandle regions.

Having known Bruce for about thirty years, mostly through involvement with various conservation issues, I had never gone salamander hunting with him. So, after arrangements were made, we embarked on a fall morning and headed west of Tallahassee down Highway 20. Cypress trees were beginning to turn golden and the purple spires of Godfrey's blazing star gave color to the piney woods along the route. Bruce started to fill me in on how a boy raised in Alaska grew to love Florida. "When I finished high school in Anchorage," he began, "the only college available was in Fairbanks and it was ungodly cold there, fifty or seventy below. In Anchorage, thirty below was the coldest. And in winter, I hardly saw the sun. So I went as far south as I could get."

In 1960, he took a job in Ft. Lauderdale driving gasoline tank trucks. He saved money and eventually moved to Tallahassee and enrolled at Florida State University where he began to develop an appreciation of North Florida's natural environment. He felt there was no money in biology, however, so he focused on math and physics. Even so, he often ventured outdoors with friends to find snakes and other creatures. He took a Vertebrate Biology course with Dr. Henry Stevenson and "just ate it up."

"Henry tried to talk me into biology as a career," Bruce recalls. "I resisted. It was the money thing. But he got me a four-month summer job banding birds in a cloud forest in Panama. One morning as I was opening up the mist nets, a huge migration of army ants marched through and I watched how the many creatures scurried away and how birds would follow them and feed on the insects that were scared up. I loved it. After the ants passed through, I lay down on the forest floor and gazed at the forest canopy overhead. It was the first time I really evaluated my value system. It was then that I realized that I had to do what I loved, not just do things for money. I suddenly felt I had lost six years of my life, so I feel I've been scrambling to make up for it ever since."

Bruce eventually earned a doctorate degree studying salamanders. Since then he has published more than 260 scientific research papers, contract reports, and popular articles. He's been the coauthor of two books and the sole author of another, and he's helped with several documentaries. He worked a stint as director of the famed Tall Timbers Research Station on the Florida/Georgia border and later founded the Coastal Plains Institute, which he still heads. Through his popular field courses, he's taken hundreds of students and lay people through swamps, pine forests, carnivorous plant bogs, river bottomlands, and unique habitats called steepheads, trying to instill an appreciation of North Florida's incredible biodiversity. "This area has the highest number of frogs, snakes, and turtles in the United States and Canada and the most salamander families in the world," he is quick to point out. "Plus, it probably has more carnivorous plants than any similarly sized area on the planet."

For our first stop, Bruce wanted to show me the place where his salamander studies began. As we headed north from Bristol, we passed numerous pine plantations where even rows of thickly planted sand pine trees seemed endless. "This used to be great indigo snake habitat," he said, sighing, "but most of the photosynthesis in these densely planted pine plantations is in the canopy— very little is reaching the ground. So, there's almost nothing growing beneath the trees. It's nearly devoid of plants. Animals such as gopher tortoises need green ground cover, and indigo snakes primarily spend nights and winters in gopher tortoise burrows. As a result, the indigo snake is pretty much wiped out in the Panhandle."

We parked along the highway where we could see the leafy canopies of hardwood trees through the spindly pines. I quickly grabbed my camera as Bruce took off toward the hardwood trees. Bruce is a large man, six foot four and 200-plus pounds. In his late sixties, he moves like someone half his age on a mission. Brush, vines, and branches are mere impediments to push through. His high school football experience comes in handy in the wilds. I scrambled to keep up. He paused on the edge of a precipitous slope that dropped 100 feet or more. We could almost walk across the tops of magnolia, beech, and tulip poplar that were rooted at the bottom and along the sides. "This is the Big Sweetwater Creek Steephead," he said proudly. "I first came here in 1962 or '63. My whole career in Florida started here, in the Garden of Eden."

A Bristol preacher once claimed that this 35-mile stretch of bluffs and ravines along the Apalachicola River was the original Garden of Eden, and it's been called that ever since. Many of the plants and animals are so unique that it is regarded as an Eden-like environment by visitors and researchers.

Steepheads, Bruce explained, are like three-sided box canyons that have small springs and clear streams at the bottom. The streams from various steepheads join together and eventually empty into the Apalachicola River, about five miles away.

Descending into the steephead, cascading dirt before us, Bruce cautioned, "This is the only place I know where black widow spiders make nests in branches. Be careful what you grab." I couldn't keep from grabbing saplings on my way down since the sharp angle of the slope was 45 degrees or greater. I slipped more than once on fallen leaves.

About halfway down, Bruce casually added, "I've found rattlesnakes down here, and this is great copperhead country." The Apalachicola River valley is one of the few places in Florida where the southern copperhead snake thrives. For a herpetologist like Bruce, it's just another biological attribute to relish.

A shady coolness greeted us as we immersed ourselves in the tropical-like habitat at the bottom. The sweet aroma of large-leafed star anise permeated the air. The man-sized evergreens framed a paradisiacal environment of clear spring water, lush ferns, liverworts, and mossy rocks. It was a naturalist's dream world, especially when Bruce dropped to his knees and began turning over large limestone rocks. "Look, here's one," he cried with almost child-like wonder, gently catching a squirmy salamander in his big hands, "an Apalachicola dusky." Bruce described the three types of salaman-

Salamander expert Bruce Means shows off two rare salamanders in a ravine near the Apalachicola River.

ders found at the head of these steepheads, the Apalachicola dusky, southern two-lined, and red. They thrive in water that is an almost constant 68 degrees Fahrenheit and never stops flowing, even during droughts. The Apalachicola dusky is the rarest. It is only found in deep ravines of the Apalachicola and Chattahoochee river basins. And like many salamander species, these creatures have no lungs; they breathe through their skin.

Rare Apalachicola dusky salamander in a deep ravine along the Apalachicola River.

We found a cluster of tiny white Apalachicola dusky eggs on the underside of one rock with a female dusky standing guard. A larger male lurked nearby. I asked what she would be protecting her eggs from. "Most definitely from the male dusky," Bruce said. Other salamander predators include snakes, raccoons, opossums, and screech owls. Bruce was careful not to disturb the female. "I didn't know they bred so late in the year," he commented. We were visiting during mid-October and Bruce thought most breeding occurred from April through September. He took some photos. "You're witnessing a scientific discovery," he said.

We followed several branches of the steephead. Bruce explained that over time, the steephead has cut inland from the river for more than five miles, and it continues to move at a glacier-like crawl. He pointed to trees that once grew along the slopes and have since toppled into the ravine. "I've witnessed movement of about ten feet in forty years," he said. "At some point in the future, this steephead will begin cutting into the road."

On our drive to our next biological hotspot in the region, Bruce explained that most of these unique environments south of Torreya State Park were unprotected when he began exploring them. He tried to get the state to buy the land without success, but when the Nature Conservancy came to him in 1980 and said that a large donor wanted to buy a unique chunk of land for conservation and asked if he knew of a good candidate, Bruce jumped at the chance. He guided conservancy representatives and the donor, Elizabeth Ordway Dunn, through the ravines and steepheads of the region and "she fell in love with the place."

At the time, a 1,200-megawatt coal-fired power plant was being proposed atop Alum Bluff, in the heart of the ravines region. But conservation officials persuaded power plant officials to relocate the plant, and Ms. Dunn was able to purchase a large area of bluffs and ravines—including Alum Bluff—through the Conservancy for $1.2 million, the largest cash contribution for conservation in Florida up to that time. Ms. Dunn also worked with Conservancy staff and consultants to establish a trust to continue funding purchases in the region. Another trust set up by Ms. Dunn allocates grants for land conservation and environmental programs throughout the state. She passed away in 1984, but her gifts continue to give.

After driving up and down tall hills that are the closest thing to mountain driving in Florida, Bruce parked beside the clear sand-bottomed Sweetwater Creek. He pulled a potato rake from the back of his pickup and I followed as he waded up the creek. "Cottonmouth moccasins like to sun along the banks," he said, "but it may be too cool for them today. They're very sensitive to temperature changes." Still, I scanned the shores as we sloshed through the cool water, not knowing how well the moccasins' inner thermometers were working.

Bruce veered off the main creek bed and began slogging through thick black muck. He stopped and began raking away debris. "This is the type of place where we can find the one-toed amphiuma," he said. An amphiuma is an eel-like salamander that looks like a cross between a snake and a giant earthworm, except that most

Bruce Means searches for amphiuma salamanders near the Apalachicola River.

Bruce Means with rare one-toed amphiuma near the Apalachicola River.

common amphiuma in the Southeast have four tiny vestigial limbs and two toes on each foot. The rare species that Bruce found in this creek only has one toe on each foot, thus the name, the one-toed amphiuma.

After several attempts, Bruce found a wet and wiggly one-toed amphiuma, about as wide as a pencil. This species was smaller than the limbed "mudpuppies" or "waterdogs" my friends and I found in a Tallahassee Creek while in middle school. The one-toed amphiuma primarily feeds on earthworms, small beetles, and larval aquatic insects. After admiring a creature that rarely sees bright sunlight, Bruce released it in the dark muck.

There was more to see, so with Bruce leading, we forged ahead up a side stream. The watercourse eventually gave way to a dry ravine as we crunched through the fallen leaves of a thick hardwood forest. While some hikers carefully step on logs to avoid snakes that might be lurking underneath, Bruce rolls them over looking for snakes, a decades-long habit, I presumed. We saw none.

After a mile or so, Bruce found a rare torreya tree. Its dark green, waxy needles fanned symmetrically on either side of a spindly trunk. The torreya, along with the similar-looking Florida yew, grows naturally nowhere else in the world.

The torreya tree dates back to 100-million-year-old fossils found in the southern Appalachians, a time when reptilian dinosaurs dominated the landscape. As climate and sea levels changed, and mass extinctions wiped out the dinosaurs and many other species, plants such as the torreya found refuge in the deep ravines and steepheads along the river. Close relatives are found in eastern Asia. "Biologically, this area is more like eastern China than anywhere else," said Bruce. Once cut for fence posts, each torreya tree is now struck down by a fungal blight before it reaches maturity, threatening this rare species with extinction. Bruce surmised that the fungus was accidentally introduced by people.

Other trees along our hike included the tulip poplar, pyramid magnolia, and Ashe magnolia, species more commonly found in southern Appalachia. Several seed varieties may have floated down the Apalachicola from the Chattahoochee, the river being the only Florida watercourse with mountain origins. Or, like the torreya, northern plants and animals may have once dominated North Florida during the ice ages and eventually became isolated in the cool ravines when glaciers retreated and warmer species began to dominate. In all, 22 northern plant species now thrive in the Apalachicola bluff and ravines area along with northern species of spiders, insects, snakes, and salamanders.

The needle palm was another common plant along the ravine. Sharp needles protect its base, but protecting it from what? The largest native herbivores are deer, and they generally browse on grass and leaves. Bruce said the answer lies in the past. "Ten thousand years ago, large herbivores such as mastodon and giant sloth roamed the landscape," he said. "Those sharp needles represent ghosts of evolution's past."

We climbed a tall sand ridge that Bruce said should have been covered by longleaf pines and wiregrass. Instead, dominant trees included holly, pignut hickory, sourwood, wild olive, sand live oak, and southern magnolia. Bruce theorized that the steep ravines and creeks that surrounded the ridge protected it from sweeping wildfires, creating a type of biological island. It allowed for the hardwoods to dominate. "I took Edward O. Wilson here several years ago," he began, "and within three minutes he cried 'Formica fusca!' He had found a species of ant that he had never seen south of Tuscaloosa, Alabama, more than 180 miles away."

The key to being a good biologist or naturalist, I was learning, was the honing of keen observation skills and having a curious mind. All life forms, from the smallest ant to large carnivores, had unique qualities and evolutionary history that could elicit a sense of wonder and discovery. And there is another trait that has become increasingly necessary in this age of rapid human population growth and hunger for resources, and that is to become an advocate for the species and natural systems being studied or appreciated. It's why Bruce worked to protect the Apalachicola bluffs and ravines system, and why he has long championed causes such as improving management practices on public lands such as the Apalachicola National Forest.

In 40 years, Bruce has witnessed species such as the five-inch flatwoods salamander being pushed closer to the brink of extinction as a result of intensive silviculture practices. A case in point was a large flatwoods salamander population south of Bristol along Florida Route 12. In the early 1970s, on rainy nights in October and November, Bruce drove the route to witness the annual migration of egg-laden flatwoods salamanders to breeding ponds across the road. He would see up to 200 salamanders on a 2.7-mile stretch of road, becoming the first scientist to document the amphibian odyssey and witness the time of year for breeding. "Everyone had assumed they bred in midwinter, not the fall," he said. Heavy rains following the passage of a cold front evidently stimulated the breeding migrations. After breeding, the salamanders would recross the road to the forest edges and savannahs on the west side, where they would often burrow into the earth.

The breeding ponds on the east side of the road were part of the Apalachicola National Forest, while the pine flatwoods and savannahs on the west side were owned by the St. Joe Paper Company. When St. Joe clear-cut, roller-chopped, and bedded their land to plant a new crop of pine trees, Bruce's rainy night drives during breeding season turned up one flatwoods salamander. One. Evidently, the habitat had changed too dramatically for them to survive. Bruce said it was happening throughout their range, especially on private commercial lands.

In order to protect another concentration of flatwoods salamanders from facing a similar fate, Bruce and I left the Apalachicola bluffs and ravines and drove farther west on Highway 20. A hearing was scheduled that evening in Pensacola, sponsored by the U.S. Fish and Wildlife Service, concerning the highly endangered reticulated flatwoods salamander. When genetic and biological data proved that the flatwoods salamander differed on either side of the Apalachicola River, the species was divided into two species, the frosted flatwoods salamander and the reticulated flatwoods salamander. In this case, a private four-lane toll road from Pensacola to Panama City was proposed to be built through the largest breeding habitat of reticulated flatwoods salamanders left in the world, on the Eglin Air Force Base.

For people who cared about the survival of all species, even salamanders, it was a call to arms. Our first order of business was to unite with other environmental advocates, so we stopped at the Nokuse Plantation near the small settlement of Bruce, a privately owned 48,000-acre tract of conservation land purchased by M. C. Davis and Sam Shine. A team of biologists were restoring the land and building an environmental education center, and allowing for thousands of gopher tortoises threatened by development to be relocated on the premises. Once at the headquarters, we met with resident herpetologists Dr. Matt Aresco and Bob Walker, along with visiting herpetologist John Palis. John and Bruce are considered to be the foremost authorities on the flatwoods salamander. They made a formidable team.

We all drove to the hearing together in Matt's van. If you didn't want to hear about the plight of salamanders, turtles, and other reptiles and amphibians, this was the wrong place to be. I got an earful. Matt Aresco in particular had been a leading advocate for protecting gopher tortoises and freshwater turtles. Thanks to his efforts, a wildlife underpass was being built beneath busy Highway 27 along Lake Jackson near Tallahassee, preventing thousands of turtle deaths.

Once we arrived at the hearing, the auditorium at Pensacola Junior College was nearly full. That's where I got an earful about the virtues of a four-lane toll road through Eglin's pristine pine flatwoods habitat. The project was the brainchild of private developers and economic movers and shakers in the region.

"If we don't build this road, we need to look at the everyday impacts on humans who have to drive on Highway 98," said transportation planner Nancy Model. "There is no long-term solution to the current traffic congestion."

A young woman named Laura added, "That salamander is a very

cute little guy, but my two children who I drive every day on Highway 98 are cute, too."

One county commissioner called Highway 98 "Bloody 98" due to its propensity for accidents. An area banker said that the toll road represented billions of dollars and thousands of new jobs. How could a salamander stand up to that?

A contract biologist named Joe Edmisten and several nonscientists claimed that the salamanders could simply be moved, a compromise everyone could live with. But this premise was disputed by Bruce, John Palis, and others. "I've been chasing after these things for twenty years," said John, "and I always hoped to find more, but haven't. Their habitat is both wetlands and uplands and very specialized. . . . You can't expect to move these things and be successful. This is the last chance to save this species."

"A lot of habitats I originally looked at are no longer there," said Bruce. He emphasized the importance of keeping the Eglin habitat intact. Otherwise, it could doom the species.

Matt Aresco pointed out that he has successfully moved gopher tortoises onto Nokuse Plantation, but in regard to the flatwoods salamander, their last habitats must simply be protected. Some species aren't as adaptable. "We have no idea what consequences might occur from wiping this species off the planet," he said. "Who knows? Maybe the salamander will provide a compound that will cure some human disease. It has happened before: Forty percent of all prescriptions dispensed in the United States are derived from plants, animals, and microorganisms."

M. C. Davis, not mincing words, simply called the private toll road idea an "ill-conceived boondoggle." The Florida Legislature had given the toll road planners eminent domain authority, and the planned route beyond Eglin cut directly through Nokuse Plantation. "Is anything sacred?" he asked.

Road advocates claimed that no other alternative routes were available since Eglin didn't want the road crossing anywhere else on the base for national security reasons. So, it was a people versus salamander debate only because the salamanders were protected under the Endangered Species Act, but what about the valuable flat-woods habitat itself and all of the other species that utilized it?

On our way home, Bruce shook his head when thinking about the many road advocates at the meeting. "These people don't realize that we're in the last days of our native ecosystems," he said. "We're replacing native species with the weeds of the world. How do you give people an appreciation for what we have lost and what we still have left in Natural Florida? You have to care about nature in the first place."

For Bruce, the salamander hunter, helping people appreciate nature and biodiversity has become an urgent mission: "I'm feeling my mortality now. Every hour is precious."

12

Mussel Power

They lack the cuteness of a salamander, the power of a panther or bear, the mystery of an ivory-bill, or the impressive navigational ability of a sea turtle. Yet, when I rub my fingers over the sculptured surface of a fat threeridge mussel, with its many grooves and ridges, I conjure up images of a raised topographic map, one that harkens back to ancient America. And to an expert like Jerry Ziewitz, this unique shell pattern points to a 10-mile stretch of North Florida's Apalachicola River and 13 miles of the adjoining Chipola River, where the world's largest concentration of these endangered mussels thrive along the sand banks.

Having Jerry as my guide on a cloudy fall day gave me an unexpected appreciation of these humble creatures that spend their lives filtering microscopic morsels from the water. Jerry works as a biologist for the United States Fish and Wildlife Service, and his job is to help document and protect threatened and endangered mussels along the river. And he has a passion for it.

"They don't have a face and they're not cute and cuddly," he said as we readied his skiff for launching near Wewahitchka. "But they do have a foot, only one—that's what they locomote with. It looks like very pale tongue. That's how they burrow."

Outer and inner shells of endangered fat threeridge mussels along the Apalachicola River.

During our boat journey downriver, Jerry rarely passed up an opportunity to continue lessons in Musselology 101. "The more you learn about them, the more fascinating they are," he said. For example, Jerry pointed out that the larval stage of these four-inch river mussels is very different than that of saltwater mussels, oysters, or clams, which broadcast their larval young into the open water. The female fat threeridge mussel sends out a web-like mass that sticks to passing fish, allowing the larval mussels, called glochidia, to attach to the gills or fins of the unsuspecting host fish. The tiny parasitic glochidia feed on the blood serum of the fish from 10 to 14 days or more before they drop to the river bottom. Most of the young mussels die in the first year, but the ones that do reach adulthood are generally long-lived, some species surviving for a hundred years or more.

If the larval mussels didn't hitch rides on fish, they could disperse only in a downstream direction with the current. The host fish are not noticeably harmed in the process, but they eventually develop an immunity that prevents mussel larvae from clamping on a second or third time.

For our first stop, Jerry took me to a mostly dried up side channel known as Swift Slough. We climbed over logs and tromped along the sandy bottom, finding several dead mussel shells. "I first came here in the summer of 2000 and found 17 fat threeridge in this slough after several hours of searching with several other biologists. In the summer of 2006, there were thousands."

During high water events, water rushes through Swift Slough to a tributary known as the River Styx. Jerry believes that high flows associated with Hurricane Dennis in the summer of 2005 moved a large amount of sand and with it a large number of mussels into Swift Slough. Having filled in with about a foot of sand, Swift Slough became disconnected from the main channel during a period of low flows in 2006, leaving the newly arrived mussels without vital flowing water. "We once had so many yellow flags marking the locations of endangered mussels in here that it looked like a Chinese New Year's celebration," he said. "But most of them perished. They need flowing water and this has become an intermittently flowing stream. They mostly move up and down, not laterally, so they were trapped."

Jerry pointed out that water would have to flow in the Apalachicola River at a minimum rate of about 6,000 cubic feet per second (cfs) or more to keep mussels in Swift Slough alive. Cubic feet per second is a standard method to measure the rate of water flow in rivers across the United States. But the United States Army Corps of Engineers, which manages dams on the river system that begins with Lake Seminole near the Georgia border and extends northward to a series of dams and reservoirs on the Chattahoochee and Flint rivers in Georgia and Alabama, could not maintain such a flow level. The demands for upstream water from farms, power plants, and cities such as Atlanta are too great, and the average rate of flow in the Apalachicola River has been dropping for decades.

The minimum flow level that the Corps seeks to maintain is 5,000 cfs, a benchmark established long before three different mussels were declared threatened or endangered in the Apalachicola-Chattahoochee-Flint River Basin in 1998. Still, because mussels

Biologist Jerry Ziewitz stands in a slough area along the Apalachicola River. Endangered mussels were once plentiful here before the area began drying up as a result of low water levels.

such as the fat threeridge receive federal protection, they are caught up in a tri-state water war that has raged for several years with no end in sight. Upriver politicians have styled the debate as "people versus mussels." A prime example is a quote by United States Congressman John Linder in the *Wall Street Journal.* Linder represents several fast-growing counties near Atlanta. He said the Corps "behaves as though mussels are more important than our children and grandchildren."

"It's easy to pick on mussels," concludes Jerry.

In reality, power plants such as a coal-fired generating station at Sneads in North Florida and Dothan's Farley nuclear plant also need at least 5,000 cfs of water for cooling purposes. Then there are the oyster beds of Apalachicola Bay. They need a minimum amount of fresh water along with periodic pulses of high water volumes coming down the river. More than 90 percent of the oysters produced in Florida come from this productive estuary.

Low water levels in the river mean that there are higher salinity levels in Apalachicola Bay. That opens the way for marine predators such as the oyster drill to come in and begin wiping out oyster beds, causing economic hardship in commercial fishing towns such as Apalachicola and Eastpoint. The City of Apalachicola has filed lawsuits to keep more water flowing in the river, and many in Florida see endangered mussels as one more weapon in their arsenal to guarantee minimum flows. In the meantime, demand for fresh water in the Atlanta area continues to grow, and the Chattahoochee River is its main water source. Farmers in the tri-rivers basin also use a tremendous amount of water, especially since center pivot irrigation systems were installed in the 1970s and 1980s. Prolonged droughts, such as in the late 1990s and in 2006 and 2007, exacerbate the problem. "It's a lot like the Everglades," said Jerry, "competition for scarce water."

If water drops too low in the river, say, to 3,150 cfs, recent studies estimate that 84 percent of the endangered fat threeridge mussels would be high and dry, and these would likely die if the condition persisted for more than a few days. "That kind of event could send these guys over the edge to extinction," said Jerry. Two other protected mussels in the river would also be impacted: the Chipola slabshell and the purple bankclimber.

Although a minimum flow of 5,000 cfs in the river keeps most of the mussels wet and the power plants working, periodic high flows that spread out through the wide floodplain are also necessary. These flood events draw organic nutrients from the floodplain to help feed the food chain, especially in Apalachicola Bay. Traditionally, the Apalachicola River's flood stage is in late February and March, but factors such as climate change and upriver water use have been affecting the natural pulse cycles of the river.

Jerry motioned for us to board the boat again to find some live mussels along the river. In recent years, he has found sites that sup-

Research team searches for endangered mussels in the Apalachicola River.

port tens of thousands more fat threeridge mussels than previously suspected because he figured out their favored habitat. "They are usually on the side of the river that is not eroding and is receiving some sand and silt deposits, but not huge amounts, like you get on the major sandbars," he said. "These places are almost always marked by young willow trees."

He took me to one such site. A group of five researchers led by Dr. Mike Gangloff of Auburn were using a small dredge to capture mussels in scientific transects so that a more accurate count of threatened and endangered mussels can be determined. In this spot, most of what was showing up in the nets at the end of the dredge pipe were small clams of Asiatic origin known as *Corbicula*. These exotic species now number in the millions along the river system, although it is not known how much they might be harming native mussels.

Jerry Ziewitz probes for rare fat threeridge mussels in the Apalachicola River.

"Let's go where I know we'll find lots of fat threeridge," Jerry suggested. As we motored upriver, he pointed out the stretches of willow that marked shores that harbored mussels. "Once I recognized the habitat for them, our known sites went from about 12 ten years ago to about 160," he said. "To find them is like an Easter egg hunt. They're not everywhere. Their distribution is highly clumped. It's really fun to find those sweet spots and see what's in them, and their life history is so fascinating."

After rounding several bends of the wide tree-lined river, we stopped beside a grove of willows and walked along the shore. Looking into the water, Jerry showed me what to look for in the soft downward-sloping bottom. A light-colored area of sand often revealed an almost imperceptible top of a mussel where they were siphoning water. He reached down, dug for a second, and gently pulled up a gleaming fat threeridge mussel. Then, he pulled up several more in the same area, along with a more common and impressively large eight-inch mussel known as a round washboard mussel.

As I joined in the search, it *was* a bit like an Easter egg hunt. I also felt like a Native American hunter-gatherer since these first Americans once harvested mussels for food. Even though the meat is highly chewy, it was an easy protein source. Plus, the attractive shells were often used for jewelry, utensils, and as a trade item. But Jerry and I didn't keep our mussel finds for a savory meal. He showed me the proper way to reposition a mussel in the sand so it can continue filtering algae, plankton, and silts from the water. A healthy mussel population can help to clean a water body, and in some parts of the world the prolific zebra mussels are introduced to do just that. However, the East European zebra mussels are considered an invasive exotic in the United States and are causing ecological problems in the Great Lakes region, killing native mussels by latching onto their shells and starving them of food and oxygen.

Besides his work with endangered mussels, Jerry takes pride in his efforts to understand the migratory Gulf sturgeon, another endangered species. In the fall of 2004, he put radio tags on about 20 large sturgeon and followed them back up the river the following spring during their spawning season. Most of the fish swam to the first dam about a hundred miles upstream, the Jim Woodruff Dam, turned around, and swam about a mile downstream, where they spawned on a large limestone outcrop. A few others spawned near

In addition to mussels, the Apalachicola River Basin harbors many other rare and endangered species. This photo was taken at Alum Bluff above Bristol.

the Interstate 10 Bridge. It was the first time anyone had found their Apalachicola River spawning areas. There are currently about 400 Gulf sturgeon of a meter or more in length who migrate up and down the river like salmon. Gulf sturgeon can weigh up to about 200 pounds and can reach impressive lengths of 7.5 feet. They once swam much farther upstream into the Flint and Chattahoochee rivers, but the dam forces them to stay in the Apalachicola.

The Apalachicola Basin harbors many other rare and endangered species, especially in an unpopulated region just north of Bristol. In the year 2000, the Nature Conservancy highlighted the Apalachicola River bluffs and ravines as a major reason North Florida was selected as one of six regions in the United States having the highest levels of biodiversity.

Though many of the Apalachicola's bluff and ravine species are rare and unique, many are not in danger of extinction because much of their habitat is protected either by the Nature Conservancy or the State of Florida. And most are not dependent upon a minimum flow of water in the Apalachicola River.

Unlike the fat threeridge mussel.

"When you have a species endemic to one system like these mussels," said Jerry, "it makes them vulnerable to catastrophic events such as severe drought, chemical spills, or untimely high flow events like hurricanes." Plus, as Jerry pointed out, anglers along the river use mussels for bait. The Florida Fish and Wildlife Conservation Commission has put together a brochure to educate anglers about mussel identification so threatened or endangered mussels are not used.

Freshwater mussels in general are among the most endangered animals on the planet. While the United States has the world's largest variety of freshwater mussels at 300 species, an estimated 70 percent are either extinct, endangered, or in need of special protection. Three species have already been declared extinct in the Apalachicola River region alone.

Threats to mussels are many. They include toxic runoff that may contain fertilizers, herbicides, pesticides and other chemical contaminants, sedimentation, dredging, channelization, dams, sand and gravel mining, and the clearing of shoreline vegetation. Other threats include competition from exotic mussels, a decline in fish species that act as hosts for mussel larvae, and unregulated or illegal mussel harvesting. Since mussels are sensitive to declines in the biological environment, they have been described as barometers of environmental quality—the water version of canaries in the coal mine—portending threats to other species and entire ecosystems.

Mussels have other important uses. Besides filtering water and eliciting gasps of appreciation from rare human admirers, they contribute to the riverine food chain by providing meals for birds, raccoons, otters, fish, turtles, and other creatures. They have thrived in the world's fresh water for about 400 million years. And even though they don't have the charisma of, say, a panther or manatee, they are fascinating in their own right and are deserving of protection.

It's time the lowly mussel gets a little respect.

13

Monkeys and Pythons

Joining a group of kayakers for a paddling trip on the Silver River near Ocala, one thing was foremost on my mind—monkeys! The river is famous (or infamous, depending on your perspective) for rhesus monkeys that were initially placed on a small river island in the 1930s by a tour operator. Perhaps the idea was to give visitors an African feel since the springs and river were being used as a backdrop to film Tarzan movies. The operator didn't realize that rhesus monkeys, native to southern Asia, are good swimmers, and so they swam off the island and habituated to the river bottomlands. They've been entertaining—and sometimes harassing boaters—ever since.

Soon after embarking from Ray's Wayside Park, the main launch spot just above the spring-fed river's confluence with the darker Ocklawaha River, I followed behind a dozen or more paddlers. After only ten minutes, we reached a bend where monkeys cavorted on both sides of the stream. While the main kayaking group continued upstream, I stayed behind with my friend Rick Poston. Rick, a third generation Miami native, has paddled the river nearly a dozen times and never tires of seeing the monkeys. "We're lucky to see so many right off the bat," he said. "There's about four troops along the river, but there may be two right here across from each other."

Mother rhesus monkey with infant monkey along the Silver River.

A "troop" (sometimes spelled "troupe") is a group or colony of monkeys.

We watched in awe as two large male monkeys got into a loud fracas with lots of screaming and biting. They took their battle to a large oak limb arching over the water. The loser was knocked into the cold water. The poor creature may have been a good climber, but he had little experience in diving. The belly flop and erupting splash made us jump. The downed monkey quickly swam to a sunny cypress root and, soaking wet, sat quietly, appearing subdued. The faces of this monkey and of many others were expressive, almost human-like.

The rest of the troop returned to their routine of climbing along trunks and branches in search of leaves and perhaps insects and small animals. Several young monkeys huddled close to their mothers. One monkey mooned boaters with a bright red behind. To observe primates outside of a zoo setting—and in Florida—was fascinating. I had seen other kinds of monkeys in Costa Rica at a distance, and that was it.

I ducked between branches and paddled to shore to take photos. This, it quickly turned out, was an error in judgment. While most native animals flee or back off when humans invade their space, the monkeys became more excited and loud. They raced toward me on branches and circled my kayak on three sides. Suddenly, I remembered stories of these monkeys, habituated to handouts, boarding boats in search of food and threatening or biting people who tried to stop them. "I'm getting out of here!" I yelled to Rick. He agreed it was a good idea. The monkeys of Silver River are best appreciated with some space between your boat and the water's edge. Humans are largely associated with food since handouts have historically been common. Feeding the monkeys is now prohibited, although some boaters can't resist breaking the law.

Wildlife officials have often viewed the monkeys as a nuisance and potential health hazard. Rhesus monkeys are natural hosts for the herpes B virus—usually fatal in humans. While the virus is normally dormant in wild monkeys, captive rhesus monkeys under stress often begin to express symptoms of the virus, posing a threat to human handlers. Just when the new state park was preparing to open to vistors, it came to light that trapped and removed Silver River monkeys were testing positive for the virus. Considering the monkeys' habit of approaching boaters for food, officials with the Silver River State Park announced that they intended to remove the monkeys from the park. The Silver Springs attraction had been regularly thinning their population for years. A local environmentalist formed a "Save the Monkeys" advocacy group and started a public campaign. A legislator and the media got involved, and a compromise was worked out for the atttraction to start a capture and sterilization program.

"Generally, monkeys shouldn't be roaming a wild river floodplain in Florida," summed up Dana Bryan, at the time chief biologist for the Florida state parks, "but we found a middle ground because of public sentiment." Bryan points out that the monkeys, in modest numbers, pose little threat to the ecosystem because they mostly feed on leaves and other vegetation. Unfortunately, the monkey population over the years tended to expand regularly until they started showing up in nearby residential communities eating dog food, at which time citizens would complain to wildlife officials. So they would call Silver Springs and the attraction would do some more thinning. And in regard to the health risks to humans, Bryan added, "All the reports of human cases of herpes B virus came from lab populations, not wild rhesus, but we were naturally worried about bites to visitors."

The tourist attraction at the Silver Springs headwaters, which now leases land from the state, is considered the primary entity responsible for the monkeys. At one point they built an enclosure for the monkeys with plans to begin a sterilization program, but the monkeys escaped. Today, in an attempt to keep monkey num-

Exotic rhesus monkey along the Silver River.

bers under control, the attraction hires trappers who periodically capture monkeys and sell them for medical research. Most land managers and wildlife officials reluctantly accept the fact that the monkeys have simply become part of the storied history and culture of the Silver River and springs, and troops will likely remain in the wild.

Not so cute are the tens of thousands of exotic Burmese or Asian pythons that are slithering across South Florida and migrating north. They may one day even prey upon rhesus monkeys and other animals along the Silver River. The infestation is largely the result of captive pythons being released by pet owners who felt ill equipped to care for them once they reached a certain size and required a steady dose of rabbits and similar-sized prey. Some owners became frightened at the growing size of their once cute pets, and for good reason. The snakes can reach up to 19 feet long and a whopping 200 pounds. Large captive Burmese pythons have been known to do more than bite the hands that feed them. Some have strangled their owners. Pythons and other exotic animals have also escaped from pet stores and owners during hurricanes.

While a handful of Burmese pythons were discovered and removed from the Everglades in the 1990s, the snake gained notoriety in October of 2005 when a state employee checking water levels in a remote canal made a gruesome discovery. A 13-foot python had tried to eat a six-foot alligator. The alligator's size and kicking legs ruptured the snake's stomach and both animals died in the struggle. Subsequent research revealed that the snakes are breeding in the wild. Since a female can lay a hundred or more eggs in a clutch, numbers are multiplying. Pythons are eating native wildlife and competing with natural predators such as federally threatened eastern indigo snakes.

A 2008 University of Florida study of feral python digestive tracts revealed a wide range of prey animals—alligator, rabbit, opossum, bobcat, muskrat, rice rat, cotton mouse, domestic cat, fox squirrel, white-tailed deer, and the endangered Key Largo woodrat. Since they are also known to frequent bird colonies, it's not surprising that six species of birds were found in the diges-

White ibis are among the species preyed upon by feral Burmese pythons in South Florida.

tive tracts, including the pied-billed grebe, limpkin, and white ibis. Endangered wood storks and other wading birds may also be part of their diet, along with the mangrove fox squirrel. No Florida panther remains were found, but it is believed that a large python could prey upon a Florida panther, and even a human. And they are slithering their way north.

"Florida's python infestation is a travesty," concluded Everglades National Park biologist Skip Snow in 2006 when the severity of the python threat was being realized. "The park is supposed to preserve habitat for wading birds and other native species, and the last thing they need is another predator."

The worst part is that thousands of Burmese pythons are still being imported into the United States each year for the pet trade, even though the World Conservation Union classified them as "near threatened" in their native Southeast Asia range as a result of capture and exportation and because people hunt them for their skins. Unmolested, a python can live 25 to 30 years.

In Florida, wildlife officials have been trained to catch pythons and exterminate them whenever possible. Since the nonvenomous snakes are nocturnal, feeding by surprise and constriction, researchers and wildlife officials have learned to wait by roadsides at dusk when the pythons come out to bask on the warm pavement. Dogs have now been trained to sniff them out. In 2006–2007, 418 Burmese pythons were captured and killed or found as road kill in Everglades National Park, up from 201 the year before and 34 in 2004.

The pythons are part of a long line of more than 130 nonnative animal species in the Florida wilds. These include iguanas, Nile monitor lizards, Monk parakeets, lionfish, boa constrictors, Gambian pouch rats . . . and rhesus monkeys. We may never completely rid the state of exotic pests, but controlling them is to our benefit, especially in regard to the Burmese python.

14

A Surge of Hope

Whenever I get discouraged about the state of the environment, nothing picks me up more than immersing myself in Natural Florida. For an easy outing, I like to stroll through the nearby Apalachicola National Forest and gaze wondrously at mature stands of longleaf pine, spotting cavities in living trees made by hard-working red-cockaded woodpeckers. The open forest makes it easy to venture off the trail and wander through expanses of tough wiregrass and blooming wildflowers. I marvel at the rich array of plant life and the sandy mounds and burrows made by gopher tortoises. Many of the plants and animals here are threatened or endangered, and the longleaf/wiregrass ecosystem is itself endangered—only 2 percent remains of its former range—but it will continue to survive as long we are vigilant, and appreciative, of what is left.

Sometimes, I strap a kayak to my car and drive a few miles to the Wacissa River. Quietly paddling along a shore of thick trees and protruding logs, snowy egrets, white ibis, and lesser yellowlegs are easy to spot against a green backdrop. Shiny black Suwannee cooter turtles slip off logs well ahead of my arrival. Little blue herons squawk their alarms. Raspy hawks cry and pileated woodpeckers punctuate the air with their high-pitched laughs. And then I

Gopher tortoises are a protected species in Florida and an animal endemic to longleaf pine and scrub environments.

hear it—a long wailing cry echoing through the bordering swamplands. It seems to speak of wildness, a call that evokes images of moss-draped patriarchal cypresses, lush green marsh grasses, and unpolluted waters. It is the speckled brown and white limpkin, also known as "the crying bird." Closely related to rails and cranes but in its own taxonomic family, the limpkin feeds almost exclusively on escargot—apple snails. Once hunted to near extinction for food in Florida, and currently a species of special concern in the state because of pollution and habitat loss, they seem to thrive along the marshy Wacissa.

On one Wacissa kayak outing, I spotted a limpkin standing on a log beside a sunning cooter turtle. I paused and watched quietly for a few minutes. The limpkin bobbed its head and neck up and down and did several short calls—not the mournful cry. More like a *kr-ow, kr-ow, kr-ow*. Another limpkin answered from across the river. The

A limpkin calls along North Florida's Wacissa River.

turtle then looked up at the limpkin while the limpkin looked down at the turtle. Their eyes locked onto each other. The limpkin emitted a clucking sound. I thought it was a wonderful example of interspecies relations as I snapped a photo. Then the limpkin abruptly poked at the turtle, forcing it off the log. Tolerance only goes so far among different species, I presumed, especially when it involves a prized log. I watched then as the limpkin probed into the water with its long bill and pulled out a gleaming apple snail; it soon pried loose the soft meat inside the brown shell and gobbled it down. Then it searched for more snails.

Long live the mighty limpkin.

If in South Florida, nothing picks me up more than a wade through the Fakahatchee Strand with its man-sized sword ferns, impressive royal palms, ghost orchids, and occasional panther tracks. The place seems to swallow me up in its wildness. Swamp water in general is a healing salve, wherever it can be found.

I have several favorite spots along Florida's coast, too, in all parts of the state. Florida has protected millions of natural acres, including several endangered beaches. One can walk barefoot on unmarred stretches of sand or kayak through mazes of marsh-lined tidal creeks or mangrove tunnels. I've come across sea turtles and manatees, sharks and crocodiles. I've witnessed the full moon nesting rites of horseshoe crabs, an ancient species, and felt forever changed.

And anytime I spot a bald eagle, sometimes while standing in my yard, I am filled with hope. We've done right with the bald eagle. In 1973, only 88 active eagle nests could be found in Florida. Now, we have more than 1,000.

The American alligator has made a huge comeback, too, from the brink of extinction to about one and a half million in Florida. I spot them on nearly every river and lake. In some places, their numbers are reminiscent of early descriptions given by William Bartram in the late 1700s. That's a testament to our protective laws and the people who enforce them.

When in need of a lift, I focus on those species that have recovered, and I remember one of the most hopeful days of my life. That's when I visited the Pelican Island Elementary School near Sebastian along Florida's Treasure Coast. In 1999, when the 50-plus fourth and fifth graders who made up the school's ECO-Troop first learned about wildlife habitat fragmentation and the challenges facing the increasingly scarce gopher tortoise and threatened Florida scrub-jay, they developed an ambitious plan. "The students came up to

2002 ECO-Troop co-presidents MacKenzie Guy and Kaitlin Thompson stand with then principal Bonnie Swanson before the Pelican Island Elementary School's protected scrub habitat.

me one day and said they wanted to buy *all* of the remaining scrub habitat in Sebastian," said then school principal Bonnie Swanson. "I almost fainted. We talked to the realtors, and they said it would take about $3 million to accomplish."

Scrub habitat primarily consists of ancient sand ridges and dunes, having once been part of a coastal island some 25 million years ago or more. The Florida scrub-jay is only found in scrub habitat, and they are Florida's only endemic bird, meaning that they are not found in any other state. Scrub-jays are mostly ground feeders of acorns, berries, insects, young frogs, and small snakes. They bury so many acorns that they help to regenerate an oak scrub forest after it has been decimated by fire, drought, or a hurricane.

Scrub habitat protected by students of the Pelican Island Elementary School near Sebastian.

Many thousands of years ago, when sea levels were much lower, scientists believe that scrub-jays moved to Florida from the desert Southwest across a wide coastal plain. When sea levels rose again, a population of scrub-jays became isolated in Florida and evolved to be different from their desert cousins. Today, the Florida scrub-jay is a threatened species with only a few thousand birds remaining in the wild.

Because Florida's scrub habitat is relatively small and becoming smaller because of the development of homes, shopping centers, roads, and citrus groves, many of the plants and animals that live in this environment are threatened or endangered. This fact is what prompted the students of Pelican Island Elementary to take action.

Learning the often difficult lesson of compromise, the students narrowed their goal to purchasing lots contiguous to 15 acres of prime scrub habitat that was already part of their school site. They first had to receive permission from their local school board, and it was no cakewalk. When one board member told the students that the school board wasn't in the business of conservation, a nine-year-old boy bravely stood up and said, "We're all in the business of conservation!" That helped to turn the tide.

Once permission was granted, the students focused on raising funds. They held bake sales and fanned out throughout the community. People were touched. Area golf course superintendents organized a tournament that raised $20,000 for the cause. Another $25,000 was donated by a local man in memory of his recently deceased wife. The initial grand total came to $65,000! But it didn't stop there. Inspired by the students' efforts, then Secretary of Interior Bruce Babbitt visited the school and awarded a grant of $218,000 from the U.S. Fish and Wildlife Service to buy additional lots.

Since development was imminent, the local Audubon Society borrowed money from a sympathetic bank to buy many of the lots until the grant money cleared. Eventually, the students purchased 17 of the adjacent lots, enough to create a park and nature trail. A sign was erected on the newly protected property: "From Us to You . . . Forever."

Scrub habitat must be maintained through periodic prescribed burning.

During my visit, students and their teachers gave me a tour of the new nature park. The habitat primarily consisted of low oaks, wild rosemary bushes, and patches of white sand. The students had been working with area biologists and were keenly aware of how to manage the tract. "We cut down some pine trees because there is only supposed to be two pine trees per acre in scrub lots," said fifth grader MacKenzie Guy. "That's because the pine needles cover the sand, and that [the sand] is what scrub-jays need to cache their food."

Kaitlin Thompson, another fifth grader, added, "We're going to do a controlled burn when the conditions are just right. The fire will burn what is not supposed to be there. The gopher tortoise will be safe in his burrow and it won't hurt the scrub-jays."

On our walk, we saw a gopher tortoise peeking out from its burrow, and spotted glimpses of blue and gray scrub-jays that make up the four to five scrub-jay families on the property. The students said that the birds were a bit skittish because the weather was windy and a thunderstorm was threatening. Principal Swanson said that when they purchased the first two lots, they came out for a ceremony so the children could sign fake deeds. "Just as they were doing this at the ceremony," she said, "scrub jays came down and landed right on the kids' heads. They're very social birds."

According to Principal Swanson, the students' efforts had unexpected consequences. By watching the children boldly advocate for something they believed in, parents and other family members began to speak up as well. The students had created a chain reaction of conservation advocacy in the area.

Warm tears rolled down my cheeks on my way home from the school, but they weren't from sadness. I felt a surge of hope. And I was not the only adult affected. "They [the students] have done things that even adults wouldn't have done or wouldn't have the courage to do or make time for," said Beth Powell, Indian River County Conservation Land Manager, soon after my tour. "They set a lot of people straight about the importance of scrub-jays here in our community. They have no problem getting up and talking in front of a roomful of adults about the scrub-jay and about what all of this means, and I've noticed that this has spread to other areas of their education."

"When I get really tired of working out in the hot sun in the middle of scrub habitat or whatever, I come out here [to the school] and get my dose of what it's all about. They inspire me."

Some months later, I read an interview with Paul Tritaik, then refuge manager for the nearby Pelican Island and Archie Carr National Wildlife Refuges. Regarding the students' efforts, he said, "They're not waiting to become adults to make a difference; they're taking action now. So in that regard, our children are not just our future, they're our present, and they can be effective as children. And to me, that's really inspiring because I remember when I was their age, I was just thinking, well, I hope some day as an adult, I can make a difference."

We need many people, all over the state, who can make a difference. That's because Florida is home to more than 600 threatened and endangered species of animals and plants. No doubt, that number will increase in proportion to sea level rise and human population growth, but rates of extinction need not rise with it. Much depends upon our elected leaders and if we can achieve sustainability at societal and personal levels. Some of our most basic choices, from the sizes of our families and homes to the types of energy and transportation we use, will affect wildlife and their habitats. All things are interconnected. What lies in balance is our future quality of life—if we can continue to enjoy Florida's incredible biodiversity—and perhaps our own survivability.

Epilogue

A Futuristic Scenario

The waning years of the 21st century are marked by dramatic change. Sea levels have risen three feet along the Florida coast as a result of melting ice in Greenland, the Arctic, and Antarctica. The Florida Keys have largely been abandoned, with much of the land inundated by sea water. What is left is more susceptible to storm surge and extreme tides. The famous reefs are diminished, leaving the island chain even more vulnerable to hurricanes and tropical storms that strike with a higher intensity than ever before. Reefs farther north, however, are flourishing.

Several wildlife species such as the Key deer, Lower Keys marsh rabbit, the Key Largo woodrat, and the Schaus swallowtail butterfly have become extinct in the wild; the only specimens that remain are housed in zoos. Wildlife officials are searching for possible re-introduction sites. The term "assisted migration" is now part of the wildlife conservation vocabulary. Some groups and professionals advocate that no species should be left behind, while others claim it is impossible or too expensive to duplicate unique habitats that are now under water. And there are other considerations. For example, what happens when Key deer are brought in contact with the closely related white-tailed deer?

The ever-growing levees and sea walls of Miami are being breached, and despite pleas for help in managing the unrelenting seas, engineers are raising a white flag of surrender. Residents are demanding a bailout from the government since their homes and businesses are of little value. Coastal flood insurance is nonexistent. Tidal inlets are wider and more numerous.

Throughout Florida, barrier islands have shrunk in size and are shifting toward the mainland. People have been retreating from Florida's coast for several years, choosing to relocate in neighboring states or in interior cities such as Sebring, Orlando, Ocala, or Gainesville and in newer communities that have sprung up on former ranchlands. Orlando has emerged as Florida's largest population center.

Sea turtles are having difficulty nesting where there are coastal levees or sea walls. They mostly utilize natural beaches that have been allowed to retreat. Where human residents are leaving the coasts, endangered sea turtles, beach mice, and manatees are expanding their range. Manatees are now wintering farther north. Plus, with fewer large boats and factory ships churning the waters because of high energy prices, the prospects are better for manatees and many other forms of ocean life. Recreational fishing, especially from kayaks and small electric-powered boats, remains popular.

The southern Everglades is transforming into a saltwater environment. Mangroves and open water have taken over vast areas once covered in sawgrass, although a restored flow of fresh water has slowed the transformation. The Cape Sable seaside sparrow is extinct. The Florida panther has lost the southern portion of its habitat. However, an assisted move north of the Caloosahatchee River and elsewhere has provided hope for its future survival.

The Florida black bear is holding on, although bear enclaves are now more hemmed in by development. Sea-level rise has reduced its habitat by nearly 10 percent. Increased upland development has caused more pressure on numerous species in the Lake Wales Ridge ecosystem near Lake Placid and Sebring, in and around the Ocala National Forest, and along the upper Kissimmee chain of lakes. As a result, a rising number of plant and animal species are considered threatened or endangered.

Some plants and animals are migrating north where there is suitable habitat and safe corridors for travel, utilizing natural areas and easements that were purchased in anticipation of the trend. Wildlife managers are constantly monitoring and trying to adapt management schemes to changing conditions. Hunting seasons are periodically being adjusted in response to warmer temperatures that have altered the timing of animal behavior. Cooperation among various agencies has proven vital in regard to research and management, and in responding to emergencies.

Florida's weather seems to alternate between prolonged droughts and intense rain events such as hurricanes and tropical storms. More intense seasonal wildfires are erupting because of higher average temperatures and low soil moisture. Pine flatwoods environments are beginning to convert to dry savannah and scrub habitats, benefiting some species and not others. Trees such as the shortleaf pine have disappeared from Florida altogether.

The higher temperatures have also allowed invasive species such as pythons and iguanas to creep northward. Several new species have found their way from Caribbean islands that are being inundated with sea water.

On the plus side, humans have succeeded in lowering their carbon emissions worldwide, although it is too late to slow the immediate effects of climate change. Still, this should help lessen the impacts of climate change in the years to come. Increasingly rare gasoline is mostly reserved for antique auto and boat shows. Air quality has improved, benefiting both humans and wildlife.

Inexpensive solar cells and high-capacity batteries have transformed the energy market. Solar cells cover most rooftops. Windmills and tidal power plants are common sights near the coast. Burning coal for energy has become expensive since only the cleanest uses are allowed. Coastal nuclear power plants such as at Turkey Point, Crystal River, and Hutchinson Island are either being phased out or relocated farther inland. The reuse of nuclear spent fuel is more commonplace, although suitable sites for the

Many barrier islands such as St. Vincent Island along the Florida Panhandle are eroding because of storms and sea level rise.

final disposal of nuclear waste are still difficult to establish. Trains have reemerged as a means to transport people and goods, often running parallel to bike paths that were built along rail lines once abandoned.

Most residents have reduced their carbon footprint by installing their own solar panels or windmills, hanging out clothes to dry, and growing more of their own vegetables. Cisterns are mandatory since fresh water is in short supply in the southern half of the state. Xeriscaping, the use of landscape plants that require little watering, is widespread, providing more backyard habitats for wildlife. Goats are increasingly being raised by people for milk and for keeping yards trimmed, and the sound of crowing roosters can be heard throughout most neighborhoods. People who have stayed in Florida have proven to be adaptive and resilient, along with some forms of wildlife.

This scenario is based upon projections by experts in various fields, inspired by the first-ever gathering, in 2008, of wildlife professionals and citizens who focused on Florida wildlife and climate change; the prime sponsor was the Florida Fish and Wildlife Conservation Commission. While some variables amount to speculation and guesswork, one thing is certain: sea levels are rising as a result of melting ice caps and glaciers, and average temperatures will rise between two and ten degrees Fahrenheit by 2100. Various scientific models differ on how fast sea levels will rise during this century. In 2007, the Intergovernmental Panel on Climate Change (IPCC) predicted a rise of less than two feet by the end of the century with a higher rise possible if polar ice sheets continue to melt at a rapid rate. The Miami–Dade County Climate Change Task Force in 2008 predicted a one-and-a half-foot rise by 2060, and a three- to five-foot rise by the end of the century as the melting of polar ice is expected to accelerate.

Some international scientists such as 2007 Nobel Peace Prize co-recipient Dr. Jean Brennan of Defenders of Wildlife and Dr. James Hansen of the Goddard Institute for Space Studies believe that a six-foot rise is possible by the end of the century because of increased ice flows from Greenland and Antarctica. To grasp this impact, consider that a six-foot rise would result in the loss of all barrier islands in the world. Ecologist Reed Noss points out that for every foot of sea-level rise, the shore of a barrier island shifts landward by 500 to 2,000 feet.

Scientists talk about a future tipping point in which sea-level rise begins to occur very rapidly. This is because ice reflects most of the sun's rays and energy, while sea water absorbs it. Once ice begins to melt, the ever-growing volume of sea water absorbs more heat, causing temperatures to rise and surrounding ice to melt even more rapidly. In polar areas such as Antarctica, melted ice water often runs down since there are no rivers on the continent. This can create fissures that cause great pieces of ice to break off and float and melt in the seas.

Lifestyle choices and the ways in which we generate electrical power will greatly influence climate change.

Of course, economic and ecological variables that we may not yet be aware of can come into play, slowing or increasing temperatures and sea levels. The most important variable, however, is how we respond to the growing threat of climate change by developing a path toward clean renewable energy and sustainable economic growth, and anticipating the changes in wildlife habitat. By helping wildlife survive, we are ultimately helping ourselves.

Bibliography

Armour, Philip. "When Pythons Attack." Salon.com News, August 18, 2006. http://www.salon.com/news/feature/2006/08/18/pythons/.

Cantrell, Elizabeth A. *When Kissimmee Was Young.* Kissimmee: First Christian Church, 1948.

Carr, Archie. *A Naturalist in Florida.* New Haven and London: Yale University Press, 1994.

———. *The Windward Road.* 1979 reissue. Tallahassee: University Presses of Florida.

Carrns, Ann. "Atlanta Is Flexing Muscles in Its War on a Little Bivalve." *Wall Street Journal,* October 26, 2007, page A1.

Cox, Jeremy. "Wildlife Group Offers Pens to Prevent Panther Attacks." *Naples News,* May 20, 2007.

Fergus, Charles. *Swamp Screamer.* Gainesville: University Press of Florida, 1998.

Finley, Wallace B. "Rarest Bird of All." *Florida Wildlife,* November 1950. Reprint in *A Florida Wildlife Magazine Anthology, 1947–2003.* Tallahassee: Florida Fish and Wildlife Conservation Commission, 2003.

Fleming, John. "Auburn group believes it has sighted ivory-billed woodpecker." *The Anniston Star,* September 26, 2006. http://www.annistonstar.com/showcase/2006/as-specialreport-0926–jflemingcol-6i26a4439.htm.

Florida Coastal and Ocean Coalition. "Preparing for a Sea Change in Florida." Booklet, 2008.

Florida Fish and Wildlife Conservation Commission. "Scientists 'Cautiously Optimistic' About Ivory-bill Evidence in Florida." News release, September 26, 2006.

Florida Fish and Wildlife Conservation Commission, National Park Service, U.S. Fish and Wildlife Service. "2007 Interagency Florida Panther Response Team Report." October 29, 2007.

Friedlander, Blaine, Jr. "News of the ivory-billed woodpecker's rediscovery thrills media, birders and researchers alike." Cornell University News Service press release, April 29, 2005. http://www.news.cornell.edu/stories/April05/Woodpecker_DC_conf.html.

Gallagher, Tim. *The Grail Bird*. Boston, New York: Houghton Mifflin, 2005.

Goodnough, Abby. "A Rare Predator Bounces Back (Now Get It Out of Here)." *New York Times*, March 14, 2006. http://www.nytimes.com/2006/03/14/science/14pant.html?pagewanted=print.

Hill, Geoffrey. *Ivorybill Hunters: The Search for Proof in a Flooded Wilderness*. New York: Oxford University Press, 2007.

Hill, Geoffrey, and Daniel Mennill. "Ivory-billed Woodpeckers in the Florida Panhandle." http://www.auburn.edu/academic/science_math/cosam/departments/biology/faculty/webpages/hill/ivorybill/Updates.html.

Hill, G. E., D. J. Mennill, B. W. Rolek, T. L. Hicks, and K. A. Swiston. 2006. "Evidence suggesting that Ivory-billed Woodpeckers (*Campephilus principalis*) exist in Florida." *Avian Conservation and Ecology—Écologie et conservation des oiseaux* 1(3): 2. [online] URL: http://www.ace-eco.org/v011/iss3/art2/.

Hulbert, Richard C. Jr. *The Fossil Vertebrates of Florida*. Gainesville: University Press of Florida, 2001.

International Whooping Crane Recovery Team. Meeting Recommendations, September 24, 2008, Wisconsin Dells, Wisconsin.

Jackson, Jerome A. *In Search of the Ivory-Billed Woodpecker*. New York: First Smithsonian Books/Collins paperback edition, 2006.

Jones, Elliott. "Scientists insist people at Round Island Park should look at, but not touch manatees there." *Florida's Treasure Coast and Palm Beach*, June 17, 2008. http://www.tcpalm.com/news/2008/jun/17/30gtplease-leave-sea-cows-in-peace/.

Larson, Ron. *Swamp Song: A Natural History of Florida's Swamps*. Gainesville: University Press of Florida, 1995.

Loney, Jim. "Florida manatee deaths decreased in 2007." Reuters, January 7, 2008. http://uk.reuters.com/article/environmentNews/idUKN0742213220080107?sp=true.

Lovett, Richard A. "Evidence of 'Extinct' Woodpecker in Florida, Experts Say." *National Geographic News*, September 26, 2006. http://news.nationalgeographic.com/news/2006/09/060926-woodpecker.html.

Malmstrom, Vincent H. *Cycles of the Sun, Mysteries of the Moon: The Calendar in Mesoamerican Civilization*. Austin: University of Texas Press, 1997.

Means, D. Bruce. "The Canyonlands of Florida." *The Nature Conservancy News*, September/October 1985, 13–17.

Means, D. Bruce, John G. Palis, and Mary Baggett. "Effects of Slash Pine Silviculture on a Florida Population of Flatwoods Salamander." *Conservation Biology* 10: 2 (April 1996): 426–437.

Mendenhall, Matt. "Historic ranges and 21 reported sightings of Ivory-billed Woodpeckers since 1944." *Birder's World*, August 2005. http://www.birders world.com/brd/default.aspx?c=a&id=471.

Mongabay.com. "Ivory-billed Woodpecker sighting may be a mistake." March 14, 2007. http://news.mongabay.com/2007/0314–ibwo.html.

Mormino, Gary. "When Panthers Stalked Florida." *Tampa Tribune*, November 9, 2008. http://www2.tbo.com/content/2008/nov/09/tr-when-panthers-stalked-florida/.

Mott, Maryann. "Invasive Pythons Squeezing Florida Everglades." *National Geographic News*, October 28, 2005. http://news.nationalgeographic.com/news/pf/98788414.html.

National Park Service. "Climate Change and South Florida's National Parks." 2007 report.

National Wildlife Federation and Florida Wildlife Federation. "An Unfavorable Tide." Booklet, June 2006.

Nietschmann, Bernard. *Caribbean Edge*. Indianapolis/New York: Bobbs-Merrill, 1979.

"On the Ground: Florida's Eco Troopers Make the Grade." *Defenders*, Fall 2006. http://www.defenders.org/newsroom/defenders_magazine/fall_2006/on_the_ground_floridas_eco_troopers_make_the_grade.php.

Perrine, Doug. *Sea Turtles of the World*. Stillwater, Minn.: Voyageur Press, 2003.

Pittman, Craig. "China Gobbling Up Florida Turtles." *St. Petersburg Times*, October 6, 2008.

Prokopiw, Romana. "Ivory-Billed Woodpecker: A Schrodinger's Cat of Extinction and Conservation." Carus Publishing Company, March 2008. http://findarticles.com/p/articles/mi_qa4136/is_200803/ai_n25138816/pg_1.

"Q & A With: Paul Tritaik, Refuge Manager." *EcoFlorida*, Summer 2003. http://www.ecofloridamag.com/archived/paul_tritaik.htm.

Quote DB website. Carl Sagan. http://www.quotedb.com/quotes/2789.

Rudloe, Jack. *Search for the Great Turtle Mother*. St. Petersburg: Great Outdoors Publishing, 1995.

Tanner, James T. *The Ivory-Billed Woodpecker*. Mineola, N.Y.: Dover Publications, 1942. Reprint, National Audubon Society, 2003.

Trivedi, Bijal P. "'Magnetic Map' Found to Guide Animal Migration." National Geographic News 10/12/2001. http://news.nationalgeographic.com/news/2001/10/1012_TVanimalnavigation.html.

United States Fish and Wildlife Service. "Biological Opinion on the Corps' Revised Interim Operations Plan (RIOP)." Report, June 2008.

———. "Endangered and Threatened Mussels in the Apalachicola-Chattahoochee-Flint Basin Involved in the Biological Opinion." Report, May 2008.

———. "Environmental Assessment for the Interagency Florida Panther Response Plan." Report, March 2008.

———. "Florida Panther Recovery Plan, Third Revision." Report, January 31, 2006.

———. "Red-cockaded Woodpecker." Fact sheet, January 2008.

Interviews

Belden, Chris. E-mail correspondence, 2008.

Bryan, Dana. Telephone conversation, 2009.

Eason, Thomas. Ocala National Forest, 2004.

Fleming, Elizabeth. Telephone conversation, 2008.

Folk, Marty. E-mail correspondence, 2008.

Hill, Geoffrey. E-mail correspondence, 2008.

Land, Darrell. E-mail correspondence, 2008.

Lotz, Mark. Naples, 2003.

———. E-mail correspondence, 2008.

McCown, Walt. Ocala National Forest, 2004.

Means, Bruce. Florida Panhandle, 2008.

Nesbitt, Steve. Gainesville, 2003.

Powell, Beth. Sebastian, 2002.

Swanson, Bonnie. Sebastian, 2002.

Thompson, Laurilee. Titusville, 2002.

Williams, Steve. Telephone conversation and e-mail correspondence, 2008.

Ziewitz, Jerry. Wewahitchka, 2008.

Index

Page numbers in italics refer to llustrations.

Doug Alderson of Tallahassee has won two national and one Florida award for his magazine articles. He is the author of four books, two with the University Press of Florida: *Waters Less Traveled: Exploring Florida's Big Bend Coast* (2005) and *New Dawn for the Kissimmee River: Orlando to Okeechobee by Kayak* (2009). His first book, *Waters Less Traveled*, was the North American Travel Journalists Association runner-up for Best Travel Book of 2006. He works as the Florida Paddling Trails Coordinator for the Florida Department of Environmental Protection's Office of Greenways and Trails. To learn more about his work, log on to: www.dougalderson.net.

DATE D